FRENCH REVOLUTIONARY WARFARE
FROM INDOCHINA TO ALGERIA

The Analysis of a Political and Military Doctrine

PRINCETON STUDIES IN WORLD POLITICS
Number 6

FRENCH REVOLUTIONARY WARFARE FROM INDOCHINA TO ALGERIA

The Analysis of a Political and Military Doctrine

PETER PARET

Published for the Center of International Studies
Princeton University
by
PALL MALL PRESS
London and Dunmow

Published in Great Britain in 1964 by
The Pall Mall Press Limited
77–79, Charlotte Street, London W. 1,
and Dunmow, Essex

Printed in the United States of America

Acknowledgments

The subject of this study has interested me from the time I became acquainted with advocates of revolutionary warfare during a stay in France in 1958. Experiences there led to my first discussion of *guerre révolutionnaire* in the *Journal of the Royal United Service Institution*. Since then I have profited from conversations with numerous French officers, antagonists as well as adherents of the doctrine, and from talks with some of their Algerian opponents. Among the persons who assisted me without ever having taken part in subversive wars, I must mention Brigadier John Stephenson, OBE, Director of the Royal United Service Institution; Colonel Yuval Ne'eman, Israeli Army; my editor, Phyllis Freeman; and my colleagues Richard A. Falk and John W. Shy. The manuscript was completed in the fall of 1962 as part of the investigation of contemporary forms of conflict carried on by the Center of International Studies; I am especially grateful to the Center's Director, Klaus Knorr, for his encouragement and support. I also acknowledge a debt to Frank Wisner II, now of the United States Foreign Service, who wrote his Princeton Senior Thesis "Algeria:

The French Army and Revolutionary War" under my supervision, and with whom I enjoyed a long and fruitful exchange of views on the problems treated in this book.

Princeton, N.J.

Contents

FRENCH REVOLUTIONARY WARFARE
FROM INDOCHINA TO ALGERIA

Chapter **1**

Introduction

Shortly before the end of the Fourth Republic, Colonel Charles Lacheroy, a well-known writer on subversive warfare and head of the French Army's Service d'Action Psychologique, recounted this parable to a meeting of reserve officers:

"Imagine, if you will, that we are sitting in on an international conference which each year decides the defense policy of the West and surveys the latest developments in military strengths and nuclear weapons. The debate of the seventeen member-nations quickly turns into a dialogue between the two sole possessors of the atom bomb—the British and the Americans—while the French representative rather absent-mindedly taps on the table.

"When he is asked to state what he thinks of the decisions taken, he replies: 'Nothing.'

"The brilliant assembly is amazed. 'What, General, you have no opinions?'

" 'No,' he answers, 'but I didn't mean I have nothing to say. I meant that the subject you've been discussing doesn't interest me. I should like to say something to you, and in obedience to the

Anglo-Saxon tradition of being lighthearted when dealing with serious problems, I will act out my message in the form of a skit. All by myself, I'll show you the reactions of Bulganin and Khrushchev, who have just heard of our international conference.

" 'Says Bulganin to Khrushchev: "Well, they've had a nice little war game over there; only, who cares about the atom bomb, it will never be used anyway."

" ' "That's right," says Khrushchev. "We'll never use atom bombs, but they have taken the very serious decision of using them on us if we attack."

" ' "Who cares about that?" says Bulganin. "We'll never attack them."

" ' "What!" shouts Khrushchev. "We'll never attack them?" We become traitors? Betray Lenin? Betray the spread of Communism across the world?"

" ' "Don't worry, we're not betraying anything. There will still be war. But because we are Communists, because we understand Communism and its laws, we have overtaken the West. We know how to fight a war that will never reach the nuclear level. We'll use every trick in the book, and let others do the fighting for us. There's no reason why the war should be waged under the Red flag. And naturally, we'll try to hit the targets that seem most promising: to begin with, the links in the chain of the French and British colonial empires." And Bulganin adds, "In this type of war, we have an unexpected advantage: Our most powerful opponents, the Americans, will be our allies." ' "[1]

These somewhat labored words, and their speaker, provide a number of reference points that are basic to any survey of the doctrine of French revolutionary warfare: its indebtedness to Communist theory; its implicit belief that contemporary events—such as anticolonialism—can be understood only in the light of a worldwide Communist conspiracy; its ties with colonial warfare, and the effort to make colonial experiences applicable to all violent and

nonviolent international conflicts. In the person of Colonel Lacheroy, who for several years was a power in Algeria until the abortive
military coups of 1960 and 1961 led first to his transfer and then
to a sentence of death *in absentia,* a further bench mark is added:
the deep, extraconstitutional involvement of the French theorists
of revolutionary warfare in the political life of their country.

To explore these areas, and bring them into true relationship
with one another, is the task of the following pages. They do not
provide a historical account—the fighting in North Africa and the
Army's political adventures are referred to only to illustrate the
workings of the doctrine—but its bearing on recent history is obvious. The Algerian War, French policy in NATO, the continuous
attempts by the Army to control government policy, cannot be understood without some knowledge of what *guerre révolutionnaire*
is about. From the mid-1950's, the doctrine provided the theoretical framework for France's effort to retain Algeria and increasingly
shaped over-all defense policy. Until very recently, it played a
considerable role in the nation's internal affairs, a realm in which
its force is not yet spent. But the doctrine's significance is not limited to France and Algeria. Despite its shortcomings, it does offer
one of the most coherent and detailed analyses yet formulated in
the West of what may be called unconventional, sublimited warfare—subversion, insurrection, and revolution—whose tools lie at
the opposite end of the spectrum from rockets and the hydrogen
bomb. In our present strivings toward a more balanced concept of
national security, and with our new—if sometimes exaggerated—
interest in unconventional military methods, we ought not to ignore the theses of *guerre révolutionnaire,* nor their implications in
fields other than the purely military.

It is striking how little serious study has been devoted to a trend
that during the past decade cut such a wide swath across military
and political France. Even now research appears to concentrate on
French actions in North Africa rather than on the ideas behind

them. This may be due to a suspicion—common in England, somewhat less so in the United States—of theory as such; to a feeling that abstractions tend to complicate what is self-evident, or worse, that they have nothing to do with reality at all. No one can deny that this instinct is often justified. But it would be equally mistaken to ignore the fact that others are less pragmatic in their ways than we pride ourselves on being; that abstractions are taken seriously both by governments and by peoples.

Perhaps, too, the purposes of military theory are sometimes misunderstood. Surely it cannot be its function to create a body of rules for all eventualities. According to Clausewitz, theory, especially when it deals with the grand strategic lines of conflict, should provide us with a methodical way of looking at events, not with an algebraic formula for action.[2] It should help us to distinguish and evaluate the elements that make up the amorphous confusion that is war. In short, the role of theory is to educate our judgment, not to press it into fixed channels.

In time, theories may lead to programs for action; but even these, once adopted, should remain subject to analysis and change. Few things in war can be as costly as doctrinal rigidity. That even the most pragmatic nations may succumb to this danger is demonstrated by such a recent episode as the systematic destruction by Allied bombers of German and Japanese cities. Certainly in the struggle against the Algerian rebels, a stubborn obedience to the tenets of revolutionary warfare blinded many French officers to the real elements of the conflict. But their errors, and the exceptional cruelties of the war in North Africa, should not inhibit an objective evaluation of the doctrine, whose misconceptions may be as instructive to us as its insights.

The concepts of *guerre révolutionnaire* were initially formulated by officers whose experiences in Indochina led them to seek new ways of countering anticolonial insurrections. The pioneers of the doctrine had all served in Asia. General Lionel-Max Chassin, whose book *La conquête de la Chine par Mao Tsé-Toung (1945–1949)* appeared as early as 1952, commanded the French Air Force against the Vietminh. Colonel Lacheroy held a staff post during the campaign; General Nemo, at that time still a field-grade officer, commanded a battalion. The junior officers among the theorists—Hogard, Poirier, Souyris, to name some of the more prominent—had served as platoon leaders or intelligence, civil-affairs, or propaganda officers. The principal lesson these men drew from the French defeat was the conviction that an inferior force could outpoint a modern army so long as it succeeded in gaining at least the tacit support of the population in the contested area. The Vietminh and their Chinese Communist backers further showed them the strength generated by a truly unified politico-military command—a demonstration borne out by the experiences of many French officers, who themselves had simultaneously commanded a unit and administered a sector. Finally, they discovered new political strategic implications in guerrilla warfare, and became convinced that proper psychological measures could create and maintain ideological cohesion among fighters and their civilian supporters.

In their learning process, the early theorists did not proceed with objectivity. They were naturally less interested in understanding the complex origins of the Indochinese War than in gaining insights that could be turned to operational use. For the sake of their argument, they assumed a flexible, fanatic opponent who had outmaneuvered an army that was both naïve in the ways of subversive war and received insufficient backing from the government and people at home. Here the operational lessons that the theorists of *guerre révolutionnaire* derived from their Vietminh opponents became joined with a sense of dissatisfaction many felt with the social and political realities of contemporary France. It was this combination, at first only vaguely apparent, that was to give the doctrine its far-reaching impetus.

The Army's acceptance of *guerre révolutionnaire* was not immediate. In 1954, students at the Ecole de Guerre were still criticized by their instructors for the extent to which their service in Indochina had affected and "deformed" their judgment.[3] Two years later, unceasing propaganda and the Algerian campaign had won over an influential part of the officer corps, and the doctrine's period of domination began. Not that the services had succumbed completely. The Navy and Air Force remained very largely unaffected, and among Army officers, very many of all ranks agreed only with the tactical concepts of the doctrine, and either ignored or rejected their wider, nonmilitary implications.[4] As the future was to show, NCO's and privates were even less convinced. But despite this, the Algerian War was being waged more and more according to the principles and techniques of *guerre révolutionnaire*.

These will now be explored, first in broad outline, then in their organizational and operational details. Analyzing a body of theory that is not the work of one man but of many could present difficulties; in this instance, however, the problem hardly exists. The numerous writings by the adherents of the theory naturally show some disagreement on minor points, but there is unanimity on everything essential, and the unity of conception extended to its practical application.

Chapter 2

The Doctrine: Revolution

In its fundamental form, the doctrine of *guerre révolutionnaire,* or—as it is frequently called—*guerre subversive,* describes a conflict waged not between sovereign states, but within one state.[1] The object of the conflict, on the part of the subversive aggressor, is the assumption of governmental authority. In the age of the Cold War, when the international community can hardly remain uninterested and uninvolved in violence unfolding within any one political system, the distinction between internal and external conflict, never as absolute as international lawyers would desire, is increasingly difficult to maintain. Sooner or later, almost every insurgent party will receive external support; indeed, it may even act as the agent of a foreign power. International ramifications, however, are not the same as international war. That actual violence is limited to one country is an obvious and important difference between internal and external war. This fact also shapes the characteristics of the struggle itself, which usually differs, at least during the greater part of its course, from the forms that fighting assumes between nations. Foreign powers may support or even instigate *coups d'état,* insurrections, revolutions; but regardless of external connections, internal violence possesses its own techniques and processes.

In an effort to express as simply as possible the basic elements of this kind of war, the French military analyst Colonel Georges Bonnet has advanced this formula:

partisan warfare + psychological warfare = revolutionary warfare

To set up this equation, he argues, "is to formulate a law valid for all revolutionary movements that today agitate the world."[2]

Taken literally, the formula is certainly misleading, even if it is held to apply only to the operational realm. The fields of partisan and psychological warfare overlap, and in practice it is often impossible to separate them. The component terms are here meant to be understood in their broadest sense. "Partisan (or guerrilla) warfare" stresses the role of individuals and small groups using terror and irregular tactics, without denying the eventual importance to the insurgents of sizable, conventionally organized formations. "Psychological warfare" is implied in all violent and nonviolent measures taken *primarily* to influence the opponent, the population, and one's own forces, as well as foreign public opinion and governments. The term thus covers everything from local rumors, terroristic acts to impress the population, and propaganda to such full-scale diplomatic action as maneuvers supporting a rebel cause in the United Nations.[3] Since guerrillas and terrorists are dependent for their survival and effectiveness on the cooperation or at least neutrality and passivity of the people among whom they operate, the winning-over of the population forms an area in which the two forces overlap. Its two halves thus expanded, Colonel Bonnet's formula not only expresses the basic composition of the French doctrine of revolutionary warfare, but also directs attention to the doctrine's salient point: the complete interdependence between the violent and nonviolent features of internal war, not alone in the methods used but also in the targets chosen. Revolutionary warfare postulates an insurgent party that will direct its efforts at least as much at the inhabitants of the territory whose control is at stake as against the armed forces of the incumbent power.

In this it marks an important change from more conventional types of conflict. Generally in war—and this appears to hold true even today—the civilian population does not constitute the main, and certainly not the first, object of attention. Despite the existence of such methods as terror-bombings, it is usually thought advisable at least to deal with the adversary's weapons systems, if not with his armed forces and his war-making potential, before the population as such ought to be subjected to direct pressure. Revolutionary warfare reverses this process. As an officer wrote in an issue of a French military journal that has become a classic among the works on *guerre révolutionnaire:* "Revolutionary warfare has for its aim the takeover of power, made possible through the active help of the physically and morally conquered population, employing destructive and constructive techniques that are applied according to a definite procedure."[4] A procedure, it hardly needs stressing, that places the use of arms at the end, not at the beginning, of the conflict.

The theorists of revolutionary warfare insist, however, that placing army and people in separate categories can be seriously misleading; they are interdependent in the revolutionary's mind. The populace, according to the formulation by Mao Tse-tung that has become one of the favorite quotations of the French theorists, is for the army what water is for fish. And more concretely, "A Red army . . . without the support of the population and the guerrillas would be a one-armed warrior."[5] The conquest—i.e., securing complicity—of at least sections of the population is accordingly seen as the indispensable curtain-raiser to insurrectional war. Once the population has been schooled and organized for the revolutionary

purpose, it becomes possible to proceed to a second act—open warfare—under conditions that are unfavorable to the incumbent
power, even though its military forces may be larger and, according to orthodox standards, better trained and better equipped
than those of the rebels.

It will be useful to enter into this rather schematic analysis of
the modern revolutionary process in somewhat greater detail. According to the Army theorists, the insurgents' first move in the
fight to control the people consists in forming cells of agitation—
noyaux actifs secrets—followed by the creation of bases, by which
is meant any area, perhaps no more than a village or a country
district, whose inhabitants have been won over by the rebels and
now find themselves under their physical and psychological domination. These bases are then developed and added to until larger
"liberated" zones are created, from which more coherent military
and political operations can be launched against the government.
The whole movement has been divided by a French analyst, Commandant Hogard, into five stages.[6]

1. Propagandists and agitators set to work secretly among the
people, sound out and appeal to any resentment against the legal
authorities and against the prevailing social and economic conditions, perhaps found a club or discussion group, while taking care
not to offend local attitudes and prejudices by too blatant a diffusion of revolutionary ideology. Their task is the preliminary reconnaissance of the ground over which the main battle will be fought:
the population.

2. Once the agitators have secured a foothold in local life, they
begin to organize activists and sympathizers into groups according
to age, occupation, and interests. These groups supervise each
other and, in turn, are controlled by committees on which activists
predominate. "The individual," a French analysis of Vietnamese
subversion declared, "is enchained in several networks of inde-

pendent hierarchies . . . a territorial hierarchy . . . running from the family and the block to the interprovincial government, and associations that incorporate male and female youth groups, groups of mothers, of farmers, factory and plantation workers' syndicates . . . they could just as well include clubs of flute players or bicycle racers; the essential thing is that no one escapes from this enrollment and that the territorial hierarchy is crossed by another one, which supervises the first and is in turn supervised by it, both being overseen by police organizations and the Party. . . ."[7] Gradually a network of coordinated opposition to the regime spreads over the country; what the French in Indochina called *"pourrissement"*—"rot"—sets in. An infrastructure of propagandists, agitators, spies, and political leaders directs dissatisfied elements among the population, while economic and physical pressures are applied to intimidate the antagonistic, the neutral, and the indifferent. People grow unwilling or afraid to help the legal authorities, who may only now begin to suspect that they are engaged in a serious struggle to maintain their authority. They will, for instance, find it difficult to introduce agents into areas dominated by the subversive infrastructure, and so are deprived of essential intelligence. These "bases," on the other hand, provide reasonable security for the instigators of the manifestations, acts of sabotage, and riots that are needed to develop a climate favorable to revolt.

3. Armed bands are formed, which engage in minor actions such as ambushing a government patrol or raiding an isolated police post. Agitation, sabotage, and terror become intense. At this stage, terror is perhaps the most powerful weapon in the subversive's armory. It may be both indiscriminate and selective. A bomb thrown into a café, where both supporters and opponents of the government will be among its victims, creates as effective an aura of insecurity, and a challenge to the authority's ability to govern, as the assassination of particular supporters of the government—officials, policemen, members of certain political parties, etc.

4. Terrorism and guerrilla activity gradually compel government forces to withdraw from certain areas, and the insurgents succeed in creating liberated zones or *bases d'appui*—territory "in which the legal government has been completely eliminated and the revolutionaries have installed their own system."[8] The Communist writer Wilfred Burchett has graphically described the fluidity and ambiguity of this phase as it appeared during the Indochinese War:

> The [revolutionary] cadres helped the people set up their own resistance administration, to organize village self-defense, and gradually form a guerrilla corps. . . . When the villages had been organized for self-defense but were still subject to French raids, tax collecting, and terrorist expeditions, they belonged to what was known as the guerrilla zone, the area where guerrillas were organized but which suffered from frequent raids. These were areas of constant warfare. Islands comprised of groups of liberated villages, into which the French dared not penetrate, but which were not joined up with the solid block of the liberated area, were known as guerrilla bases. There was a constant, almost chemical process of change as pieces of occupied areas passed into the guerrilla zone category, the guerrilla zones changed into guerrilla bases, and the latter expanded and joined up with the liberated areas.[9]

Now the rebel leaders can emerge into the open and establish a provisional government—either in the base areas or abroad under the sponsorship of a foreign power—not only to strengthen their control of the people but also to gain the international advantages of legality. Governments friendly to the insurrection can now recognize it, openly supply it with arms, and act in its interests on the international stage. A regular army is organized, which further helps to transform insurrection into legitimate war. By extending their raids and acts of terrorism to the still unconquered areas, the rebels widen the rift between population and authorities.

5. The last phase consists in a general psychological, political,

and military offensive against the government and its armed forces.

The theorists of *guerre révolutionnaire* readily admit that neither this, nor any other schematic description can reflect accurately the fluidity of the subversive process. Events overlap and blend, to some extent their sequence may vary. For instance, men may band together, secure arms, establish themselves in a remote district, and only then proceed to transform it into an ideologically charged base—though it must be remembered that as long as they are not protected by the population, they can hardly prove a match for government forces. Nor have insurgents always found it necessary to proceed through all five of the stages outlined by Commandant Hogard. The organization of liberated zones, or even of strong guerrilla bands, may by itself sufficiently demoralize the government to induce it to grant fatal concessions. These and other variants, however, do not in the view of the theorists affect the general validity of the doctrine, which, they hold, correctly identifies the seeds of insurrection, and the means employed to bring it to fruition.

On one point of the analysis, and this admittedly a major one, the theorists seem at first sight to disagree. What causes insurrections and revolutions? How do they originate? To Colonel Lacheroy, the prophet of psychological manipulation, the matter is plain. "In the beginning there is nothing," he declares—"nothing," in this case, meaning the secure existence of the *status quo*.[10] This void continues until an external agency decides to fill it. As the world was created by God, so the social and political unrest of a country are brought about deliberately by an omnipotent outside force.

That such a view does not accord with reality is apparent. Conspiracies of one type or another, varying in intensity and extent,

always exist, even in situations that do not lead to general violence. They are a fact of political life; but not necessarily a determining fact. The Indochinese War, for example, which provided
the most impressive model of revolutionary warfare to the French
theorists, opened with native guerrilla harassment of the Japanese
invaders during World War II. After the Japanese surrender, and
after almost a year and a half of fruitless negotiations over greater
Indochinese participation in the government, fighting resumed in
the form of conventional operations waged against the French by
a force of 60,000 regulars. It was only when these had been defeated that clandestine organizations, parallel hierarchies, and
guerrillas emerged as the decisive carriers of action.

The more sophisticated among the theorists are cognizant of
complexities such as these, which Colonel Lacheroy's demonology
ignores. They recognize the potential for disorder that lies in the
frustrations and inequities of society itself or in political upheavals
that need no masterminding, such as the effect World War II
had on underdeveloped countries.[11] They insist, however, that
grievances and dislocations pose no real problem to the incumbent
until they are nurtured and exploited by agitators, who—directly
or indirectly—work for the Communist cause. In practice, therefore, little if anything distinguishes their point of view from
Lacheroy's. Both consider it a prime characteristic of revolutionary
war that it is waged by remote control, and both are agreed that it
is essentially ideological in nature: "There is no true war other
than religious war."[12]

Rigid and limited though it is, however, the analysis does indicate with some accuracy at least stretches of the path that internal
conquest has taken in a number of countries since 1945. Without
seriously delving into the reasons for unrest, the doctrine of *guerre
révolutionnaire* offers a useful operational analysis of the subversive process. Useful, that is, not to the statesman or administrator,

who may wish to understand and deal constructively with explosive social and political forces, but for the soldier, who wants to blunt their military edge.

The strongest feature of the French analysis undoubtedly rests in its comprehension that the intermingling of military and political factors in revolutionary movements constitutes not a mark of primitiveness and lack of development, but a source of power. The French writers never tire of pointing to the unconventionally close connection and interdependence of political, military, and psychological factors in all areas of modern revolutionary activity. No strict division, to mention once more the most obvious example, need be drawn by the insurgent leaders between their army, the guerrillas, and the civilian population among which they operate. Generally, the lack of much complex equipment and of a long administrative tail simplifies the problems of training. In a technologically underdeveloped society, it is relatively easy for civilians to pass into guerrilla formations or regular corps; regular units, on the other hand, may be assigned guerrilla duties, or may temporarily revert to civilian existence. Their mission is, in any case, only partly "military." In the Indochinese War, for example, General Nemo discerned four major areas of responsibility of the Vietminh cadres: They were a force of political and military education for the soldier and administrator; they generated propaganda throughout the population; they were an instrument of coercion against opponents of the movement; and finally, they were a tool for combat.[13] Two of the most important aspects of war, providing and transporting supplies, and gathering intelligence, lie for the greatest part in the hands of civilians, and insurgents rarely find it useful to separate military, political, and economic information.

Once the insurgents have won their first skirmishes and are beginning to be of more than local significance, their military and nonmilitary forces interact on new levels. Political problems, even those of international scale, are now perceived and solved in military terms. Of all the French theorists, Commandant Hogard has dealt most pertinently with this development:

> The revolutionary opponent obeys in tactics as well as in strategy the first of Lenin's principles of war, "the security of the rear."[14] He tries to maintain his own while destroying that of his opponent.
>
> His own are the "bases," which have sometimes evolved into "liberated zones." His techniques of controlling the population allow him to secure these easily, without assigning many troops to the task.
>
> The rear areas of his opponent are of two kinds. Those that one might call "Zone of the Interior" (for example, Metropolitan France during the Indochinese War or during the [fighting in Algeria]). To reduce them, he can call on numerous open supporters . . . and on all those whom his *mystique* of double-dealing has deceived of his true nature. Experience has shown that he can create trust in many!
>
> But he must also attack the enemy rear in the area where the war is actually going on. To achieve this, he again employs his techniques of conquering the population. If his bases are sufficiently numerous, this takes place in the framework of guerrilla action. If his opponent is materially and morally sufficiently weak, if he is dispersed, and if they can move rapidly, it is achieved in the framework of mobile warfare. Both guerrilla and mobile operations thus rest on control of the population, [and its control] in turn is brought about by [these operations]. Military action is therefore closely bound up with all other efforts, be they political, economic, social, or cultural.
>
> . . . In brief, revolutionary warfare is very different from traditional conventional war. Widely dispersed at the outset, it gradually draws strength and resources from the enemy, seeking to capture not military or geographic objectives, but the population. When the situation is ripe it concludes with a single all-out effort in which all its forces are concentrated—if this is still necessary. Generally, the last battle is won before it has started since the enemy is swamped, groggy, demoralized— he is psychologically ready to be defeated.[15]

No one can fail to recognize the Indochinese experience and behind it the doctrine and practice of Mao Tse-tung as the intellec-

tual ancestors of these paragraphs. By 1956, when Commandant
Hogard and his colleagues had crystallized these theories, they
were convinced that the superiority of the revolutionary armies—
which were never as well equipped as the French forces they
dodged, harassed, and finally defeated—was based on two factors:
the disciplined political conviction of their cadres and the conquest of the population.[16] Moreover, the struggle against contemporary insurgent movements, whether waged by France or other
nations, was likely to be of long duration and marked by a relative
absence of fronts. Their clandestine and ideological features would
always impose a heavy moral and physical strain on both sides.[17]

Chapter 3

The Doctrine: Counterrevolution

The doctrine of *guerre révolutionnaire* deals with two major areas of conflict. One—the nature, characteristics, and processes of modern revolution—it treats haphazardly and, except in its study of the tactics, with little sophistication. The other area, which covers the principles and techniques of waging war against revolution, it has closely and elaborately explored. To understand one's own policy more clearly than that of the enemy is a common condition of military affairs. What is striking in the case of *guerre révolutionnaire* is that its detailed concept of counterrevolution is taken directly from its vague view of revolution; the reflection in the mirror is sharp, while the thing reflected remains shadowy.

The theorists of *guerre révolutionnaire* recognize that unless the over-all and local superiority of the incumbents is of an exceptional magnitude, a successful answer to internal aggression must contain a large share of nonmilitary measures. Purely military techniques of control will suffice in some cases—in Tibet, for example, or perhaps in South Africa—but there are at least as many cases where simple repression cannot succeed. In either type of situation, the incumbent's efforts should of course be directed at the weak points of the subversive process. These, according to the doctrine, are:

1. Insurrectional war assigns a pre-eminent role to psychological warfare. Its use "is based on the sense of good and evil innate in every human being . . . if the revolution wishes to succeed it must pervert this moral sense." The superiority of the ethical code of the West, which is assumed by these theorists, should give it an advantage over the enemy, as long as it shows equal aptitude in the use of psychological warfare.[1]

2. The early development of subversion—the progression from propaganda to the first tentative raids—requires a great deal of time. The enemy forges his weapon under the eyes of the legal authorities and can only hope that security forces do not interfere before he is ready.

3. At the outset, the insurgents scarcely ever possess an adequate logistic base, though neighboring countries friendly to their cause may go far to make up this deficiency.

4. The insurgents can draw out the struggle for very long periods, but are almost never able to deal decisive military blows.

5. Most important, the conquest and control of the population, which is an indispensable condition of success, is based on the existence of an infrastructure, the clandestine politico-military network of cells, activists, and sympathizers covering the country. If this organization of ideological elites is broken up, the war collapses.

These are serious weaknesses that offer excellent opportunities to the incumbents. But even if exploited sufficiently and in time, they may not lead to complete victory. Indeed, some French writers have argued that the incumbents can never achieve such an outcome in revolutionary war. Commandant Hogard has charac-

terized the wish for complete victory as a delusion, which only in-
terferes with the conduct of operations.[2] If the insurgents should
fail in their guerrilla or regular campaigns, if they should be forced
to withdraw from their liberated zones, they can easily enough revert to the earlier phases of insurrections, to relatively limited military and political activity. The best the incumbents might hope
for is to restrict the insurgents to the establishment of cells, to the
spreading of propaganda, to a degree of sabotage and terror that
can be accepted by the government and society.[3] To the obvious
query whether an attack on the political, economic, and social
motives of the insurrection might not prove a government's most
effective strategy, the doctrine has an unequivocal and negative answer: It would be dangerous to confuse the will of an organization
that sets off the struggle, and pursues it, with the internal contradictions and inequities of society. The former is the real, the latter
only the pretended, cause. According to this interpretation, the
Algerian rebellion, to take one example, was not born of Moslem
discontent with political and economic inferiority; the real cause
lay in the wish of Cairo and the FLN to chase the French from
North Africa. It would thus be pointless to expect that reforms,
even if joined with conventional military and police measures,
could end the insurrection. That the mass of the people may be
dissatisfied and wish for change is not denied; but it is argued that
the revolutionary elite fights either because it is committed to a
particular ideology or for personal power.

This approach to revolution logically results in a conclusion
that may be considered the fundamental concept of the doctrine:
It is a mistake to think that revolutionary war can be won by negotiation. The rebels are not interested in ameliorating conditions, in partial victory. Negotiations, by helping them consolidate
their position, only accelerate the process that leads to their capture of total power.[4] However, the doctrine continues, once the
incumbent government recognizes the treacherousness of negotiations, regards reforms as a useful auxiliary to pacification—but as

no more than that—and renounces the hope of ever being able to stamp out all opposition, it should be well placed to exploit the weaknesses of the insurgents.

During the early stages of an insurrection, while the level of violence is still low, it is relatively easy to prevent further deterioration by an energetic effort to educate public opinion, coupled with necessary reforms, with repression by the police, administration, and the courts, and by Army control of the danger zones. Prerequisites for effective action are an alert intelligence service and a government that recognizes the gravity of the threat and is willing and able to meet it.

If the insurrection has not been contained, and the rebels manage to reach Commandant Hogard's third, fourth, or fifth stage in the revolutionary process, the government's task becomes infinitely more complex. Again, its military, political, and psychological efforts should be closely meshed:

1. The rebels must be cut off from foreign assistance.

2. The enemy's regular forces and larger guerrilla groupings must be destroyed. This can never be an aim in itself; it is useful primarily to the extent to which it helps in the more important task of breaking up the rebel infrastructure. The Army's measures must therefore be guided as much by political and psychological considerations as by military ones. The tactics employed should be inspired by guerrilla warfare; every success should be exploited by psychological operations aimed at fostering demoralization and desertion.

3. Communications and essential administrative and economic centers must be protected; but the armed forces must not be tied down to this duty, which is really useful only if it is followed by measures leading toward the control of the hinterland and its pacification. These two tasks can best be accomplished by spreading and augmenting a network of small posts over the area. Their commanders should be aware of the cardinal need to win over the

population, to educate or re-educate it, and if possible to induce it to take an active part in the fight against the insurgents.

4. It may be necessary to undertake resettlement of communities, perhaps even on a large scale, in order to deny these potential bases to the enemy and at the same time to facilitate their supervision and protection.

5. Finally, the captured rebels should be re-educated.

Action and successful reaction in revolutionary war might be plotted as follows:

INSURGENT

1. Formation of propaganda and agitation cells.
2. Expansion and coordination of opposition; riots, sabotage.

3. Intensified propaganda; terror; minor armed actions; guerrillas; diplomatic activity.
4. Creation of liberated zones; installation of provisional government; gradual change from irregular to regular warfare.
5. Regular warfare; fully developed diplomatic activity.

4. Regularization fails; reversion to guerrilla war.

3. Reduction of liberated zones; small-scale guerrilla war.
2., 1. Propaganda; agitation; sabotage; terror.

INCUMBENT

Police and intelligence activity; strengthening of military and administrative controls; propaganda; social, economic, and political reforms.

Mobilization of the state's physical and political resources; attack on the subversive infrastructure; organization of self-defense units; education and re-education programs; resettlement of population; reconquest of liberated zones; isolation and destruction of enemy forces; diplomatic activity.

Reduction of the regular and auxiliary military effort; continuation of reforms and re-education; evolution of a new order.

Underlying this waxing and waning of effort on both sides must be powerful ideological and moral forces that bind separate techniques into a dynamic strategy. The writers on *guerre révolutionnaire* are in little doubt over the nature of the insurgents' motivation. It is either Communism, or a Communist-inspired movement, or an irresponsible nationalism that easily lends itself to Soviet exploitation, a category that takes care of such cases as the eight-year-long Algerian War, in which Communists played an insignificant role.[5] And even these distinctions are dismissed as academic. In 1957, in an address at SHAPE that remains one of the most important high-level statements of the strategic and tactical concepts of *guerre révolutionnaire,* a French corps commander, General Allard, claimed that the Soviet Union

... has concealed from many the fact that the direction of her main effort was not the East-West axis, but a vast enveloping curve passing through China, the Far East, Southeast Asia, the Middle East, Egypt, and North Africa in order to encircle Europe.[6] This is now almost a reality, the one step remaining is to wrest Algeria from France.

To wrest it from France under the pretext of the people's right for self-determination, fostering a myth of nationalism and independence to create a new Arab state incapable of fending for itself, to turn it with its eastern and western neighbors into the spearhead of Pan-Arabism, all this means preparing the ground—here as everywhere else —for Communist takeover and satellization. France had earlier attempted to stem Communist expansion in Indochina . . . the free world did not understand the importance of these attempts, and they failed. Our last, our ultimate line of defense is Algeria.[7]

If figures such as General Allard or Jacques Soustelle insistently identified "the Algerian War as part of a great world struggle against Communism,"[8] it is not surprising that officers in the field would dismiss the Algerian fellagah as a "Viet," and take his Communism for granted. It would nevertheless be a mistake to read too much into statements that were at least partly motivated by the needs of propaganda. The theorists of *guerre révolution-naire* recognized that the FLN fought for a cause; they might label the rebel ideology Communism or Pan-Arabism, but its exact analysis mattered far less to them than the creation of an equally effective counterideology.[9]

What could be the great idea that would bring life to the French counterrevolutionary effort? In Indochina, it is safe to say, such an idea had been lacking. To many professional soldiers, that defeat had clearly demonstrated that conventional patriotism and *esprit de corps* were inadequate weapons against revolutionary *élan,* particularly if—as they claimed—the government neither understood nor sufficiently supported the fighting. It was a point of view that refused to accept the concept of limited war, and that overlooked or discounted the numerous errors which the Army itself had committed. The French Army, these men insisted, would fight the next war under different conditions. Two changes were called for: Government and nation had to give complete support to the armed forces, and these forces themselves had to experience revolutionary changes in their concepts of duty and ethics as well as in their tactics.

When the Algerian rebellion broke out, in 1954, these aims were far from achieved, indeed they had scarcely yet been formulated in detail. Nevertheless, from the outset, a greater measure of cohesion existed among the French than among the Algerians, and the military weakness of the insurgents gave the French Army additional time to evolve the necessary moral driving force.

Five major factors combined to produce this ideological motor. There was, to begin with, the determination to regard Algeria not as a colonial possession or protectorate, but as a part of France not to be ceded under any condition. Though by no means universally held even among regular officers, this feeling was widespread and powerful. At the same time, despite its genuine force, the concept of *Algérie française* had some of the characteristics of a program designed for the outside world, a façade that covered other motives of at least equal significance.

A vocal and influential minority of officers had begun to lose faith in the standards and performance of French society, and was on the search for new and more potent ideals, for what the French sociologist Raoul Girardet described as "an international doctrine capable of effectively opposing Marxist-Leninist theories . . . a system of values strong enough to unite and stimulate national energies." The search took the soldiers on many roads. In 1959, in the most sophisticated apologia for *guerre révolutionnaire* yet to be published, Girardet summarized their efforts in these terms:

> Some, perhaps the majority, will attempt to define an ideology based on the exaltation of the traditional values of Western humanism: the dignity of man, patriotism, respect for spiritual values, the desire for justice and progress. . . . Others overtly express their espousal of the principles of a strict type of Catholicism, finding the answer to the revolutionary menace in the establishment of an authoritarian, traditionalist Christian order which explicitly repudiates the postulates of liberal individualism. Finally, others lean towards an anti-Marxist, as well as anticapitalist, national collectivism. Needless to say, there is much confusion and hesitation, along with many contradictions, in this systematic quest for a doctrine.

Rather wishfully, M. Girardet concluded that "the mere existence of the quest is more significant than the results it produces; it does not presuppose political commitment on the part of young officers; it does not involve any militant action from within a party or group"[10]—a deduction wholly disproved by subsequent events.

Indeed, the officers who seriously accepted the tenets of *guerre révolutionnaire* had to acknowledge that its counterrevolutionary program could not be adequately implemented in a multiparty, liberal France. The nature of operational methods constituted only one of the problem areas. Equally incompatible was the need to impose onto the various regimes a policy of full support for the war; the Army had to enter politics on a grand scale. But in an ideological struggle, even governmental support was insufficient if the nation as a whole refused to become involved.

> From now on [an anonymous senior officer declared in 1956], Frenchmen must unite behind their Army. Whenever the Army has sensed that all of France stood behind the military effort, victory was achieved. It will be again, if the Army regains the deep conviction that wars undertaken to preserve the integrity of the *Union française* are truly national wars. Frenchmen must behave in a manner that gives the Army this conviction.[11]

But the degree and kind of ideological solidarity which the theorists so admired in the Chinese and Indochinese Communists, and which they felt could be defeated only by a similar moral force, was impossible to achieve under the Fourth or even the Fifth Republic. These were the considerations that prompted Commandant Hogard to assert as early as 1958 that "it is time to realize that the democratic ideology has become powerless in the world today."[12]

A "combative system of values strong enough to unite and stimulate national energies" was a prerequisite for the successful prosecution of the war against the FLN; it was needed equally to regenerate the moral fiber of metropolitan France. The search for a combative ideology thus became intimately tied to a sense of mission. Not only was Algeria to be saved from Pan-Arabism, France itself was to be saved from inefficiency and corruption, and turned into a disciplined, progressive power. In the eyes of the theorists and adherents of *guerre révolutionnaire,* the war in Algeria became part of a greater crusade for the spiritual and national future of France.

Reinforcing these spiritual longings were considerations of a more conventional military nature. The fear General Allard expressed of Europe's flank being turned in the Mediterranean was at least an arguable strategic concern. Joining it was a matter of professional pride and interest that weighed heavily with many officers who were left untouched by the more grandiose aspirations of the theorists. Since 1945, the Army had retreated wherever it fought—in at least one case, Suez, after turning in an outstanding performance. The war against the FLN offered the Army a final chance to regain its confidence and reputation.

Finally, the Army's insistence on winning in Algeria perfectly suited the interests of numerous civilian groups in North Africa and metropolitan France. These circles gladly turned to their own use the energies of the evolving doctrine. The Army, more and more deeply enmeshed in politics, was only too exposed to this kind of exploitation, and by 1960, at the very latest, was no longer capable of separating its own idealistic and professional concerns from the very different motives of its civilian allies.

But the uprising of May 13, 1958, the "Week of the Barricades," the terror campaign of the OAS, still lay in the future. By 1957, the counterrevolutionary ideology had crystallized out of a combination of political concerns, strategic and professional interests, hatred of Communism, a desire to remake France. The result possessed neither the simplicity of nationalism nor the universality of Marxism, and it entirely lacked the realistic tactical appraisal both made of the contemporary world. It remained stunted, hamstrung by contradictions, advocating policies that were far in excess of the actual power at its disposal. But if the ideology was inadequate, its operational message was clear and unambiguous.

The Army, it declared, was engaged in a permanent world-wide revolutionary conflict in which the differences between anticolonialism, non-Western nationalism, and Communism were insignificant, and in which the traditional distinctions between war and peace had disappeared. The Algerian battlefield occupied a key position in this conflict. Here the main enemy effort was directed at winning the support of the civilian population, at breaking down the morale of the French forces and administration and, by extension, of the nation itself. This total attack called for a total response. Not military power alone, but all means at the disposal of a highly developed society had to be committed. The war, furthermore, could end only with the effective—if not total—defeat of the enemy; negotiations, compromise, the acceptance of limited goals could only damage one's own cause. This rigidity was also necessitated by tactical considerations: An idea of such appeal as independence could be countered only by a concept as all-encompassing as integration. The crusading ideology thus had a fateful effect on the Army's operations. The insistence of the theorists and adherents of *guerre révolutionnaire* on a total politico-military effort, the rejection of compromise, pushed the Army more and more deeply into positions that were untenable politically as well as militarily.

The incumbent's response to insurrectional war according to the doctrine of *guerre révolutionnaire* has been outlined. How was the program to be implemented in the field? General Allard, in his speech at SHAPE which has already been cited, divided the methods used in Algeria into two categories:

> In revolutionary war, pure military action, which is of first importance in conventional war, takes a back seat to psychological action, to propaganda, to the collecting and exploiting of political as well as operational intelligence, to police measures, to personal contacts with the population, to social and economic programs, etc. . . . A complex program must be carried out, in coordination with a small-unit war, over an area of some 350,000 square kilometers (not counting the Sahara). I shall classify these various missions under two categories: Destruction and Construction.
>
> These two terms are inseparable. To destroy without building up would mean useless labor; to build without first destroying would be a delusion.
>
> 1. *Destruction.* This means first of all to uncover, dismantle, and suppress the rebel politico-administrative framework, the nerve center of the rebellion. Through it, the mass of the population—willingly or more usually by force—is taken in hand, separated into groups, indoc-

trinated, pressured, terrorized—caught by one means or another in a tightly meshed net from which there is no escape.

To open this net, to destroy this many-tentacled organization, means giving the people back its freedom, liberating it from moral and physical constraint, ridding it of a paralyzing cloak of fear. This mission constitutes our first objective. It is more in the nature of a police action than of a military operation. It requires the cooperation of all legal forces under a single command: the Army, the police, and all intelligence agencies.

Destruction further means to chase and annihilate the armed enemy bands, that is to say, the guerrilla units, which do not form the rebellion's nerve center but one of its means of action. The guerrillas are the fists of the rebellion; their task is to deal spectacular blows against the legal forces (ambush is their favorite tactic), to maintain insecurity, to demonstrate the rebellion's power to the people by constant threats and frequent actions, by bloody exactions, and to fake the impression of a whole army. . . .

This mission to destroy the bands, essentially military in character, assumes the form of antiguerrilla operations with all the difficulties this implies in a country that consists largely of rugged, mountainous terrain, often thickly covered with forest.

It requires a great deal of manpower, much of it scattered over the countryside, in combined units (with air support) but containing a heavy preponderance of infantry.

2. *Construction.* Destruction will achieve nothing if we don't go beyond it. If the population were left to itself, the rebel organization would soon emerge again. After having destroyed, we must construct.

To construct means building the peace, preparing the establishment of a new order. This is the task of pacification. It calls first of all for the re-establishment of personal contact with the people; we must protect and help them in every area, and thus give them back the confidence they had lost or were losing in the grip of the FLN. Pacification also means organizing the people, separating them into hierarchies, that is to say, substituting for the political and administrative organization of the FLN new groupings beginning at the lowest echelon of the future [social and administrative] organization of Algeria. . . .

Finally, construction means to persuade the population by the use of education, the establishment of self-defense systems, and the setting up of native auxiliary combat forces (harkas) to collaborate in the fights against the rebellion. . . .

These extremely diverse missions of the Army are very far removed from those that normally fall on armed forces in a conventional war. But at least they offer the French Army the opportunity of understanding the contemporary realities of small-unit war and of revolutionary war.[18]

For purposes of operational analysis, General Allard's categories of "Destruction" and "Construction" may be further broken down into three groups—destructive techniques, politico-psychological techniques, and constructive techniques—forming three phases of a closely integrated program that found its most complete expression in the "Plan Challe" applied to Algeria between 1958 and 1960. The analytic breakdown should not suggest a sequence in time; in Algeria, implementation of the three was often simultaneous, or nearly so, with the emphasis moving from one area of effort to the other. The first phase, carried out by the combat forces and police, aimed at the destruction of the politico-administrative organization of the revolution and of its armed units. The second phase had the dual objective of destruction and construction; it sought to annihilate the ideological commitment of the people to the revolution, and to establish a new ideological and political base on which the counterrevolutionary order could be built. Under the third or constructive phase, the needed political, social, and economic reforms were carried out, the population organized into a new social and administrative system, and persuaded to join actively in the fight against the revolution.

The next two chapters discuss the components of these phases: Chapter 6 will analyze an example of their cooperation in the field.

Chapter 4

The Components of Counterrevolutionary Warfare

Destruction

Even before the French authorities recognized that the Algerian insurrection had grown beyond local significance, their repressive measures aimed at the twin goals of isolating the disturbance and of wearing down its armed power. The change from police action to open warfare did nothing to alter these underlying operational principles, though now they had to be implemented on additional fronts. Intercepting arms shipments off the North African coast was a relatively simple matter. On the international scene, the French Government maneuvered with some success to limit diplomatic recognition of the Nationalists. It proved more difficult to deny the FLN refuge in neighboring countries. Diplomacy did not succeed in persuading the governments of Tunisia and Morocco to disarm the rebel contingents training on their soil. Armed retaliation, of which the bombing of the Tunisian village of Sakiet was only the most prominent example among many, resulted in little military gain, while costing a great deal in diplomatic complications and unfavorable public opinion. More effective was the attempt to close the Algerian borders against FLN incursions from Morocco and Tunisia. Along the Tunisian frontier, the Morice Line—two rows of electrified fencing and barbed wire, separated by minefields and strengthened by radar and blockhouses—ran from the coast some 200 miles south to the Sahara. During the day, scouting planes flew overhead; at night, the line was lighted by floodlights and patrolled by tanks and armored cars; held in reserve were mobile units able to repel major breakthroughs. A similar, though not equally extensive, system guarded the Moroccan frontier. To increase the effectiveness of the barriers, the population was evacuated from certain adjacent areas, and the land designated forbidden zones where civilians could be shot at sight. The numbers of Algerians involved were considerable. For example, 300,000 Moslems in the Constantine area, along the Tunisian border, were transported to 250 settlements farther inland.[1] The cleared zones gave the Army a free hand; operations carried on here were purely military in character, not—as frequently elsewhere in Algeria—guided by political and social considerations.

To the end of the war, the frontier barriers successfully inhibited the Nationalists' use of sizable regular formations. The land blockade compelled the FLN to wage a guerrilla struggle with fragmented bands that lacked secure rear areas where men could rest, train, and be re-equipped. Command and supply problems were intensified, as was the serious division in the rebel leadership between commanders in the field and the provisional government and its representatives in Egypt, Tunisia, and Morocco. On the other hand, the barriers did the FLN a service by removing the temptation to regularize the conflict prematurely—to fight conventionally in large formations before possessing strength, equipment, and expertise to do so effectively. Essentially, the barriers were a passive measure and, therefore, inadequate. They could neither reduce the foreign sanctuaries without which the rebellion might well have withered, nor destroy the insurgents' regular forces, which, though immobilized on neutral territory, performed important functions as an "army in being," helping, for example, to give Algerian nationalism an air of permanency and international respectability.

The French handicapped the concentration of rebel forces inside Algeria by covering the greater part of the country north of the Sahara with a grid or checkerboard of garrisons and fortified posts. The effectiveness of this network of close territorial control, called *quadrillage*, depended largely on the thorough local knowledge each post could acquire, and for this reason, troops were given permanent assignments whenever possible. Their responsibilities included routine security, police work, collecting and evaluating intelligence, constructing roads and strongpoints, and limited operations against the rebels. They were backed by mobile units whose mission was "to destroy the enemy's politico-military organization . . . to regroup the dispersed populace to ensure their protection, and to organize them so that the inhabitants participate in their own defense."[2] Larger offensive operations were entrusted to forces of intervention, the Reserve Générale, elite formations of paratroopers, marines, mechanized infantry, legionnaires, and helicopter units. In the later stages of the war, about 300,000 troops were committed to territorial defense and 30,000 to the Reserve Générale.[3] This combination of static territorial control and mobile forces of interception had a long tradition in the French Army, having been employed against the Royalist uprisings during the French Revolution, in nineteenth-century colonial campaigns, and to some degree in Indochina.[4] Against a widely dispersed guerrilla movement, its advantages were considerable.

The first prerequisite in fighting against an irregular opponent, obtaining a constant flow of detailed military and political information, could be satisfied only by establishing widespread personal contacts with the population. Mobile forces lacked the time, training, and inclination to mingle with crowds, but soldiers who lived in a village for years learned to read the local atmosphere, particularly if they had orders not to isolate themselves in their barracks. Their constant and knowing presence handicapped the rebels, and in this war, the saying went, the discovery of an FLN messenger or middleman was as important a victory as the capture of a fort had been in more conventional conflicts. Besides keeping count of the local pulse, the garrisons were to represent to the Algerians the image of a strong but benevolent and progressive France. As a Chief of Staff of the Army later explained it: *"Quadrillage* attempted to put French troops—to the last man, to the last private—in direct contact with the Moslems, turning each into a kind of ambassador to the Moslem population."[5]

From a purely military point of view, implanting small garrisons across the country led to a balance and permanency of control that the French could not have achieved by grouping forces in a few cities and strategic centers, or by launching massive but necessarily temporary operations. An officer explained how the concept operated in the past:

> economy of force meant accepting weakness in one place in order to be strong in another. Economy meant "successive equilibrium." In subversive war, on the contrary, we believe that economy of force means "permanent equilibrium," that is to say, a distribution of strength that allows the "simultaneous" execution of all missions. . . . If an important engagement takes place at A, it will be useful to detach 10 or 15 battalions from C, D, and E . . . [but] if I were to send 20 battalions to A, the advantage I might gain there would not compensate me for the resulting imbalance suffered by the over-all mission.[6]

But despite their numerical superiority of more than 10 to 1, the French found permanent equilibrium impossible to achieve. Often a dozen guerrillas tied down companies; the high command never had at its disposal the manpower to implement fully both the tasks of *quadrillage* and of pursuit and destruction—and modern arms, radio communications, and helicopters, while useful, proved an inadequate substitute. The division of duties in the forces incidentally created a difficult morale problem. Local garrisons, performing dangerous but dull and unglamorous tasks, came to resent the elite formations that fought the major battles and then returned to their bases, well publicized and decorated. The mutual dislike that arose between paratroopers and the ordinary conscripts had important consequences when Army factions assumed the role of national arbiter in 1960 and 1961.

Mobile operations changed their character in the course of the war. Up to 1959, reliance was officially placed on large-scale maneuvers of encirclement—*bouclage*—and on great sweeps or drives with extended fronts—*ratissage*. It is doubtful whether these constituted the most effective response to irregulars. Forces of division or corps size could be concentrated only at the risk of denuding other parts of the country, and their necessarily slow assembly could not be hidden from the FLN. Tactical surprise, too, tended to disappear with the use of large numbers and heavy equipment. Although the guerrillas suffered considerably in these near-conventional operations, they were flexible enough in tactics and organization to avoid total defeat. Long before the disappointing outcome of the last attempt at a massive victory—"Operation Precious Stones" in the Kabyles—emphasis had shifted to the small unit, striking at carefully reconnoitered targets, sometimes with the added mobility of helicopter transport and parachute drops. The elite formations primarily entrusted with these missions were supplemented by special counterguerrilla detachments, drawn both from French and Moslem regulars and from native auxiliaries. Particularly effective were the *commandos de chasse,* groups of 60 to 80 men that attempted to copy the FLN's tactics by operating as irregulars in the country for weeks at a time.[7] General Salan, during his tour of duty as Commander in Chief in Algeria, spelled out their role as

> moving always on foot and nearly always at night, carrying out surprise attacks on well-chosen targets, unexpectedly arriving in villages, attempting to gain maximum intelligence on FLN units and arrest or eliminate rebel personnel, setting up intelligence networks, ambushing local rebel bands, if necessary splitting up in groups as small as four men . . . perhaps calling on artillery and the air force to engage sizable rebel concentrations, these units would create constant insecurity for the opponent while gradually giving the rural population a comforting feeling of constant security.[8]

Another attempt to fight fire with fire was the subversion of anti-French guerrilla bands and their employment against the FLN. As early as 1956, a dissident nationalist, Bel Hadj, known as "Kobus," was authorized to mount antiguerrilla operations in his home district around Duperré, southwest of Algiers. The group, named "Force K" after its chief, soon demonstrated considerable independence, and its failure to cooperate with neighboring French commands led the Army to introduce closer controls, including the assignment of 100 paratroopers to act as operational support and guarantors of good behavior. During 1957, "Force K" fought successfully against the local FLN, so that the Army permitted its expansion from 200 to 600 men and supplied it with modern weapons; at the same time, however, it was infiltrated by nationalist agents. In April, 1958, Kobus and some of his followers were murdered by rebel supporters, and after a running battle with French ground and air units, part of the band joined the FLN, while the rest surrendered to the French.[9]

On a larger scale, but essentially similar, was the case of the "National Army of the Algerian People," under Mohammed Bellounis, a follower of the veteran nationalist Messali Hadj, whose movement had split with the FLN. In 1957, Bellounis agreed to enter the war against the rebels in the southern Atlas Mountains in return for French arms and supplies. He gained some successes, notably in keeping Highway 1 open for the oil transports from the Saharan fields; but he also began to set up his own political network and administration in the area, and it became apparent that his political ambitions did not fit French policy. His adhesion to the French cause had been widely advertised, but by the summer of 1958, the Army felt it had no choice but to eliminate Bellounis —however damaging the publicity. He was captured on July 14, and killed the same afternoon while attempting to escape. Of his 3,300 followers, many were killed or went over to the FLN; 300 joined the government forces.

Among the numerous attempts to detach Moslem bands from the nationalist camp, only one seems to have met with permanent success. In 1957, the former French Sergeant Major Si Cheliff, who had fought alongside the rebels for two years, went over to the French with 170 men. They were assigned to a district west of Algiers, where they soon neutralized the FLN network. From the outset, Si Cheliff operated under the direct control of the authorities, who supervised the gradual expansion of his group to 600 men and integrated it more and more fully with the regular forces. For some time after May 13, 1958, Si Cheliff played a role in the movement of fraternization between settlers and Moslems, appearing in the Algiers Forum, in front of the Governor General's residence, and attesting Moslem loyalty to the French cause, until the collapse of French rule swept him under.

Promoting dissension among the nationalists was a useful policy, but the allies gained in the process were hardly reliable. The tendency to play off one side against the other appeared to be almost universal among Moslem chiefs; to keep them under control, their men had to be regularized to some extent, and with the coming of liaison officers, of uniforms and paratroopers, the bands lost the ability to blend into the countryside and merge with the population, which had been their most significant military asset.

Of greater help to the government were the tens of thousands of Moslems who joined the French singly or in small groups. According to a government report, the number of North Africans who volunteered or were drafted for service in regular units increased from 20,000 at the beginning of 1957 to 61,500 in June, 1960.[10] Moslems fighting in auxiliary units were even more numerous.

Apart from the village self-defense forces three main types of auxiliary service existed. Most important were the harkas, supplementary combat troops organized in squads with their own corporals, but commanded by French senior NCO's and officers. They were employed both in *quadrillage* duties and on mobile operations, either as commandos or more generally as part of a regular company or platoon. Usually inferior in fighting qualities were the makhzan, recruited as guards, orderlies, and messengers by the Army's civil-affairs teams. The civil administration also hired some thousands of Moslems as auxiliary policemen, the Groupes Mobiles de Securité, among whom were the Para Bleus, made up of former FLN terrorists and guerrillas. A little-known metropolitan counterpart of the GMS was a militia of Arab and Kabyle volunteers, operating under the Parisian prefect of police, whose task was to hunt down FLN members among the Moslems working in France—particularly collectors of financial contributions to the rebel cause.[11] How many men served as harkas, makhzan, and auxiliary police during the war is impossible to determine with certainty, since many were paid out of local funds and there was a high incidence of short-term enlistments. Toward the end of the war, the government released these figures on Moslem auxiliaries:

	January, 1957	December, 1957	June, 1959	June, 1960
Harkas	2,200	16,900	41,500	57,500
Makhzan	3,400	12,200	19,000	19,000
GMS	3,500	6,200	6,000	8,500[12]

Even if these are approximations, the total Moslem contribution to the French effort was considerable, amounting to perhaps 146,000–150,000 regulars and auxiliaries—more than one-quarter of the ground forces and specialist units engaged.

The recognition by the French High Command of the need to recruit the largest possible number of Moslems did not blind them to the drawbacks involved. In a depressed, overpopulated country, many Algerians undoubtedly served for the sake of regular pay and rations; their presence facilitated FLN infiltration, and they complicated the operational picture. Their reliability and loyalty were not above suspicion, and planning had to take this into account. Though many auxiliaries distinguished themselves in combat, the tendency was to use them rather for reconnaissance, for guard, supply, and transport duties. Often, guaranteeing the safety of the harka's immediate family was an essential part of the recruiting bargain, and in some cases the Army had to go to the expense of building protected compounds for his dependents. But these problems of security, organization, and tactics could not detract from the very tangible rewards: The presence of tens of thousands of armed Moslems under the tricolor gave credence to the French claim to fight for Algeria rather than against it. Truly widespread and active public support together with flexible counterguerrilla tactics—whose very effectiveness depended on the intensity and extent of civilian cooperation—might have led to a more favorable outcome for the French. The inadequacy, lateness, and contradictions of their political program prevented a sufficient rallying of the population.

Construction

Creating and maintaining public support for French policies devolved largely on the psychological services, whose work is discussed in the following chapter. They operated in the broad and shifting area that stretched between destruction and construction and impinged on both. In addition to fortifying the morale and the ideological cohesion of their own troops, their tasks were to break down the Algerians' allegiance to the rebel cause and to promote adherence to France. Beyond these measures of propaganda and psychological warfare lay another realm of policy—constructive in intent if not always in execution—that tried to change Algerian society directly. Its basic assumption was that social change and modernization under French auspices could best bring about immunity to subversion; its primary components were the resettlement of a large segment of the population, political and administrative reforms, educating the young—both men and women—in the ways of Western technology, and capping these, the transition of militarily and psychologically vulnerable rural communities into self-defense hamlets.

Removing civilians from the border zones permitted the Army to wage uninhibited war against the rebels. Regroupment of large numbers of people in the interior joined to this conventional military motive the wish to deprive the enemy of the true object of the war. The Army, by evacuating those rural communities it could not effectively protect, was able to jeopardize the continued existence of the subversive network in the area. The rebels' sources of information, of supplies and finances, vanished, and with them their sources of recruits. As General Challe was to declare in 1961, at his trial: "The theory, the famous theory of water and fish of Mao Tse-tung, which has achieved much, is still very simple and very true: If you withdraw the water, that is to say, the support of the population, fish can no longer live. It's simple, I know, but in war only the simple things can be achieved. . . ."[13] In addition, resettlement not only hurt the enemy but also brought the population under more stringent control, and at least in theory, afforded the opportunity of restructuring and re-educating a part of Algerian society under something approaching laboratory conditions.

Once more, the war of the First French Republic against the peasant counterrevolutionaries in the Vendée presented the staff officer of the 1950's with an example imbedded in his native tradition. The orders of the Republican Army of the West in 1793 had called for the removal "from the insurgent territory [of] all inhabitants who had not taken up arms, because some, under the guise of neutrality, favor the rebels, while the others (the smaller group), although loyal to the Republic, also provide assistance which they cannot refuse in the face of compulsion."[14] More recently, certain operations against the Vietminh indicated some of the current possibilities and problems of this technique. During the 1940's and early 1950's, Vietminh infiltration in the Cambodian border provinces was undercut by relocating the widely scattered peasant population to new fortified settlements that could be defended against incursions and at the same time brought the inhabitants under more comprehensive control.[15] In Vietnam, the French—perhaps mistakenly—felt unable to carry out this scheme, which would have proved particularly difficult and expensive in a country whose densely populated arable land sharply limited the possibilities for creating new farming communities. In Algeria, however, the underpopulated *bled* made it feasible to repeat the Cambodian experiment on a larger scale. Or so it seemed; in reality, European ownership of much of the arable land precluded its use, since neither the Army nor the civil administration was willing to institute a serious program of land reform at the expense of the French settlers.

At first, Algerian communities were regrouped on the basis of local decisions. By 1957, these improvised moves had crystallized into the general policy of *regroupement* or *resserrement des populations*. This policy was implemented in three stages. Moslems were removed from vulnerable locations to areas that could be defended, and dwellings and other necessary facilities were constructed under Army supervision. Measures were instituted to turn passive and dislocated human beings into economically viable groups. Education and propaganda, the convincing evidence of French power and of French social responsibility, were then expected to win over some Moslems, eventually making possible a degree of self-administration and the active participation of the community in its own defense. Once political and military indoctrination had been completed, the symbolic and highly advertised act of handing rifles to the Moslems put the public stamp on their efficiency and on the entire community's fidelity. The home-defense groups released some troops to other duties, but more valuable was their open commitment to the French cause. Their example facilitated further conversions, while any rebel move of retaliation made a genuine *rapprochement* between villagers and FLN more difficult. "Above all it should be remembered," an officer declared after the war, "that [Challe] launched this policy of self-defense villages not so much for military reasons, but because he saw in it the only way to bring the mass of Moslems to our side once and for all."[16] Two years earlier, when a French victory could still be hoped for, a commentator wrote, "Someday historians will be amazed at the reversal of the situation brought about by the resettlement of people around certain villages that have been turned into fortresses. To some extent, Algeria is again taking on the character it possessed before the conquest, the character of feudalism. . . ."[17] Colonel Trinquier agreed: "In effect, we are reestablishing the old system of medieval fortified villages, designed to protect the inhabitants against marauding bands."[18] The social and political implications of these comparisons were left unspoken.

In what was soon to be considered a model regroupment, 300,000 people in the Blida region, southwest of Algiers, were shifted from their villages and farms and resettled into compounds surrounded by barbed wire, watchtowers, and guard posts.[19] Rebel political activity and terrorism in the area, which at times had influenced the struggle in Algiers itself, was almost wholly extinguished. But the success demanded an investment of personnel, finances, and detailed staffwork that the Army could not afford whenever regroupment seemed necessary or desirable to the High Command. Consequently, many mass moves were hurriedly planned and inadequately carried out. Of the more than 2,000,000 men, women, and children who left their homes by edict or force of circumstance during the fighting, a majority exchanged the familiar poverty of country and village life for an artificial and alien misery.[20] If their transfer eased operations against the FLN, it did little to gain adherents to the French cause. Nor was it possible to prevent rebel infiltration in the new communities. A more favorable ground for subversion could hardly be imagined than the resettlement centers, with the concentrated hatred and frustration of thousands. By 1959, the serious shortcomings of the program had grown apparent, and emphasis shifted to improving the existing settlements. The government announced that no further camps would be created, and that the *bled* would be modernized by the building of 1,000 new villages among which the dispossessed Moslems were to be distributed. The Army ignored this order and continued to resettle people in large numbers up to the truce announcement of June 17, 1961. Separating the population from the guerrilla bands of the FLN was of more immediate importance to the theorists and practitioners of *guerre révolutionnaire* than the new problems that were created among the dislocated.

The self-defense program began on a minute scale; no more than 3,200 rifles had been distributed by June, 1956. After four years of intense effort, toward the end of the war, 1,840 villages were part of the system—between two-thirds and three-quarters of the total usually considered necessary to achieve complete pacification of the Algerian countryside.[21] How meaningful these figures on pacified villages were cannot be determined. No district could ever rely wholly on its own resources for defense, and a reduction of regular troops in the area favored the resurgence of rebel operations. Such cases frequently resulted in the creation of a French-FLN condominium: The villagers reached an accommodation with the rebels, providing them with information, food, weapons, and money, while they retained their ties with the legal authorities. Nevertheless, the FLN repeatedly tried to tear gaps in the network which its leaders considered a serious threat unless its extent and effectiveness were rigidly limited. Not as an end in itself, but as a temporary measure, while more far-reaching political and / or military moves could be readied, the strategic-hamlet system had its value.

Administration, schooling, and political mobilization of the resettled Moslems were largely controlled and carried out by service personnel, grouped in teams designated SAS (Section Administrative Spéciale). The first SAS units were formed as early as September, 1955, and consisted of civil-affairs officers who had served in Morocco and in the Sahara. Their mission was, in official phraseology, "to re-establish contact with the population" in the Aurès Mountains, where the FLN had destroyed what little French administration had ever existed. The SAS was only the latest version of an organization that could be traced back almost to the inception of the second French colonial empire. In 1844, Marshal Bugeaud, the conqueror of Algeria, had set up the Bureaux Arabes to act as intermediaries between the Army and the natives, to gather political and military intelligence while operations were still in progress, and later to help secure the victory by introducing French administration and by paving the way for French commerce and colonization. Each of the 41 Sections that were eventually established possessed considerable latitude; initiative and independent judgment were demanded of the commanding officer, and their flexibility and opportunism made the Bureaux into effective agents of the pacification process. With the consolidation of civil rule, the importance of the Bureaux declined and they were gradually abolished, except in the south of the country, which was never considered fully pacified.[22] Similar politico-military teams played a role in other colonial campaigns, most significantly under Lyautey in Morocco. Their modern counterparts were integrated more closely with the operational commands, but in time many achieved an exceptional degree of local autonomy. The typical SAS unit consisted of an officer; his second-in-command—sometimes an officer, but often an NCO or even a civilian; an interpreter; military or civilian specialists in such fields as public health, agriculture, education; a radio operator; clerical help; and often a squad or more of native auxiliaries.[23] The headquarters of the unit was usually located in a compound or group of houses organized for defense; this would include an infirmary, a social center, a school, a market, repair shops, and administrative offices for the area.

The duties of the SAS, largely advisory in its early days, soon expanded. In district after district, the Sections assumed direct control of local government; they filled a void created by war, frequently attempting to balance in a short time, and with considerable effort, the administrative and social irresponsibility with which Paris had ruled Algeria for more than a century. An SAS command might build schools and staff them, run an anti-illiteracy campaign among the adult population, open an infirmary and organize traveling teams of physicians and nurses, select and train Algerians who would collaborate with the French in all phases of administration, including that of home defense. The members of the Section might plan and supervise the building of roads, try to improve the agricultural techniques of the natives, help systematize the marketing and distribution of goods, find work for the resettled population of their district. In the economic area, emphasis was placed on cheap, short-term programs that could be expected to bring quick returns; sometimes, however, the SAS engaged in large and technically complex projects, such as the attempt to reclaim land in the neighborhood of Constantine by desalination—a project to which it was driven by the French settlers' near monopoly of arable land.

Along with his economic and politico-administrative duties, the SAS officer continued to bear operational responsibilities. His knowledge of the country and of the population made him the most dependable source of intelligence for the local troops. The diversity of his duties was reflected in the position he occupied in the military and civil hierarchies. The SAS chief was independent of the local operational command, whose area of responsibility did not always coincide with his. He took his orders from the senior officers attached to the subprefectures and prefectures of the civil administration and—at least, officially—from the civil administration itself. At the same time, he cooperated closely with the local troops, on whom he was largely dependent for labor, transportation, and security.[24] A decree of September 4, 1959, which assigned the SAS officer a coordinating role between the subprefects and the Moslem mayors of the Algerian countryside, legalized his position as the representative of French administration in most immediate contact with the population. His powers of tutelage and veto led to protests even from Algerians loyal to France. To one such accusation of highhanded political interference, an SAS chief replied in a letter whose tone and content are indicative of the manner in which the SAS interpreted its mission:

> Give proof of your capacity to handle your municipal affairs without the help of the SAS commanders, and these will be the first to applaud.
>
> We are officers outside the regular Army structure, representatives of the subprefect in our areas, and thus constitute the lowest echelon of the prefectorial hierarchy. We are neither police commissioners nor combat soldiers. We are something different. Each to his own work. This truth, evident in law, becomes apparent in fact as soon as I appeal to the Algerian people, whose overwhelming majority recognizes the task of human solidarity and of the reuniting of minds and souls, the work of pacification, of the SAS.[25]

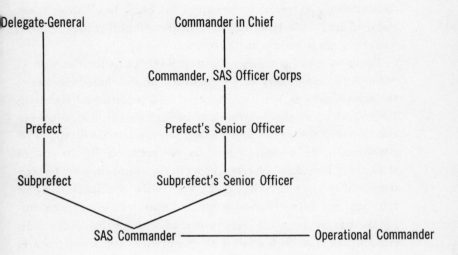

SAS COMMAND STRUCTURE

In 1957, during the battle of Algiers, teams similar to the SAS were formed to operate in the towns, the SAU (Sections Administratives Urbaines). In the towns, it was less a question of filling the administrative void than of expanding and adapting the existing organization. The SAU constituted a link between civil servants and the armed forces, and at the same time acted as an intermediary between the armed forces and the natives. It tried to provide work and housing for the Moslem proletariat and the refugees crowding the *bidonvilles* (slums), attempted to strengthen the social services, to mobilize the population for the French cause—for instance, by sponsoring labor unions—and to provide intelligence to help the Army's war against terrorism. A sister organization, attached to the metropolitan police, tried to ease the lot of the more than 400,000 Algerians working in France, and to combat the fund-raising and terror campaigns of the FLN. In all three areas, the principle underlying the work of the Administrative Sections was the same: to reform and to control.

There were never sufficient SAS or SAU teams for the tasks at hand. Although officers were recruited from the three branches of the armed services, the high personal and professional standards limited selection, the program was underfinanced, the dangerous conditions of the service and the low pay offered handicapped recruitment of the civilian specialists. Nevertheless, by the end of 1959, there were 1,287 officers serving in the approximately 660 sections, assisted by 661 NCO's and 2,921 civilian specialists.[26] Their achievements were of considerable importance to the French during the war, and in some cases proved of lasting value to the independent Algeria. In a conflict that combined the worst features of both colonial wars and civil strife, the Special Sections attempted, in the apt phrase of the British journalist Peter Partner, "to tidy up the mess of war before the war is over." They also tried to create the basis for a new relationship between metropolitan France and Algeria.

That many of their duties lay in building, teaching, and healing appealed to the idealistic and the unconventional soldier. A military elite was fostered in the Sections, whose members evinced an exceptionally intense personal involvement in their work.[27] Faith in social construction was their unifying concept, but they valued it for different reasons, and approached it from different directions. The officers who believed that the rebellion could be defeated only with political and economic weapons were joined by others who distrusted the Army's methods of pacification and above all sought to ameliorate the conditions of the people. For some, service in the SAS was a form of inner emigration, an escape from the dilemmas of a war they could not wholeheartedly support. In time, the prestige of the SAS officer became very high, though his tendency to cut across the conventional lines of command made him enemies among his comrades. Despite the divergence of motives in their ranks, the SAS also came to perform an important function in maintaining French morale. For the Army at large, and for the nation, their achievements balanced the darker sides of the Algerian War. A not unimportant secondary gain was the favorable impression their activities made on Western public opinion. In the otherwise universally unsuccessful French propaganda efforts, the SAS provided the one bright spot.

But although their operational successes were great, their long-run achievements are questionable. Even if the rebellion had been defeated, the extent to which they would have achieved their aim of building up solid adherence to France among the people seems doubtful. The mission of the SAS was compromised by certain assumptions and preconceptions that any organization of that type would find difficult to shed. The SAS officer was less concerned with understanding the Algerians than with turning them into docile collaborators. From imposing French bureaucratic control and instructing the population in French principles of public health, it was a short step to advocating French social and cultural values while—implicitly or explicitly—condemning native traditions. Far from uniting the two races, such paternalistic tactics were divisive and could easily recoil on their users. To give an example: It was understandable and yet an error that the schools organized by the SAS taught French rather than Arab history. The heroic names written on the blackboard were Jeanne d'Arc, Napoleon, and Foch—not Abd-el-Kadr and Abd-el-Krim. Children were taught to identify with alien masters and precepts that held no favorable associations for them outside the classroom. It was not surprising that they would translate the militant French nationalism they were taught into militant Arab nationalism. With the psychological-warfare services, the SAS shared the difficulty of being engaged in a conflict that was fought along racial lines, of having to win over Moslems and Berbers—whose cultural inferiority few Frenchmen would deny—to a way of life whose presumed superiorities in no way increased its appeal to strangers.

Chapter 5

Psychological Action—
Psychological Warfare

The ancestors of the French Army's psychological warfare services were the various propaganda and information services that had been formed during and after World War II. The Defense Reorganization Decree of April 1, 1950, established a central bureau responsible for these matters, placing it under the Secrétaire Général Permanent de la Défense Nationale, who assisted the Premier "in the interdepartmental coordination of measures dealing with national defense."[1] In the beginning, the Section d'Action Psychologique (SAP) was made up of a small group of civilians who had the duty of publicizing and selling government policy to the public. Their first task was to counter the Communist campaigns against the Atlantic Alliance and against the build-up of American forces in France. As AP gained experience in coordinating information programs of the ministries concerned with defense and in cooperating with its NATO colleagues, its power grew. By 1952, it had reached the status of an interministerial commission. Its duties now included working out a long-term propaganda program in support of the new defense effort and in addition, exploring techniques of social psychology. Although contact with the armed services was increasing—through courses for officers on public-opinion research and publicity, for example—the Army was not yet convinced of the importance of psychological action.[2] This skepticism ended with the Indochinese disaster.

In Asia, the French Expeditionary Corps had already raised psychological-warfare sections on an *ad hoc* basis; in October, 1952, these were brought under the supervision of the Direction Générale de la Guerre Psychologique, staffed by French and Vietnamese officers and civilians. Initially nothing more than conventional propaganda units, the sections gradually took on responsibility for a whole range of politico-military measures designed to regain control of the population. At the same time, their members began to develop a theory of unconventional warfare, which increasingly emphasized the psychological factor. The shock of successive defeats at the hands of natives—seemingly demonstrating the inadequacy of Western equipment and training—demanded an explanation, which was sought in nonmaterial forces. The failure of metropolitan France to turn the Indochinese conflict from a limited to an all-out war also led to a reassessment of the role of ideology. Moreover many officers had been personally exposed to one aspect or another of psychological warfare. Some had been subjected to re-education measures in Vietminh prison camps and, though not succumbing, had nevertheless been impressed by the techniques and strong convictions of their tormentors. Others had witnessed or taken part in French psychological-warfare operations. Many more had at times wielded both political and military authority—organizing native self-defense forces or administering a district—activities in which persuasion and propaganda had played a major role. Among the veterans returning from Indochina, there was considerable readiness to look further into the potentials of psychological weapons.

If some years of peace had followed Dien Bien Phu, military and civilian experiences might have become synthesized into a doctrine of psychological warfare not inimical to a parliamentary democracy and applied by an agency under firm governmental control. The outbreak of the Algerian rebellion, with its sophisticated exploitation of propaganda, both added new pressures and enabled the Army to dominate the field. In February, 1955, the first training center for psychological warfare was set up in Paris, followed by the provisional formation of Bureaux Psychologiques in Algeria, which were primarily intended to enlighten French soldiers on the political aspects of the war in North Africa.[3] It was a sign of the growing acceptance of psychological warfare by the official hierarchy that the Army's General Staff section dealing with morale and information was in the same year renamed Section Psychologique et du Morale. In April, 1956, the Minister of National Defense established the Service d'Action Psychologique et d'Information (SAPI), which was officially concerned with press relations, but under its head, Colonel Lacheroy, became a powerful agency for spreading the doctrine of *guerre révolutionnaire*. Courses in psychological warfare were introduced in the curriculums of the service academies and staff colleges, and an interservice center was founded to train instructors and specialists. In November, 1957, the improvised Bureaux Psychologiques were made official, being inserted as 5es Bureaux into the staffs of combat units and territorial commands.[4] According to the table of organization, the 5es Bureaux were to be headed by three officers, in charge respectively of press relations, psychological warfare, and "national affairs," the two latter being members of the General Staff, while the press officer was detached from SAPI. In fact, however, the same individual often assumed all three responsibilities. A "re-

gional bureau" of psychological action was attached to the staff of
the Commanding General in Algeria; the head of this section
joined senior civil servants on the Comité Restreint d'Action Psychologique, which formulated over-all policy and coordinated the
work of the civil and military agencies in this field. Finally, in
July, 1958, these new staff sections were capped by the 5e Section
of the General Staff of National Defense, a body that had taken
the place of the Permanent Secretariat, under which AP had begun its existence. In eight years, the psychological services of the
government had increased enormously in size and in operational
and political importance. They had changed from an advisory
board on the periphery of power into an executive organ, which
disposed of such sizable allocations of money and personnel that
it began to be called the seventh arm of the service. With little or
no exception, its key positions were occupied by proponents of the
doctrine of *guerre révolutionnaire*.

The 5es Bureaux

In the Algerian conflict, the 5es Bureaux acquired responsibility
for two tasks. One, *action psychologique,* had the far-reaching aim
of protecting French morale and unity of purpose, civilian as well
as military. In the terminology of its practitioners, it was to act
directly on the services and indirectly on the nation, though this
distinction was not observed in its efforts to mobilize the Algerian
population—Moslems being treated as much as a captive audience
as were service personnel. The other task, *guerre psychologique,*
carried the psychological war to the enemy in order to rob him of
his supporters and destroy his will to fight.[5] Three objectives were
distinguished in the work of *guerre psychologique:*[6]

1. To help destroy the enemy's political network.
2. To help destroy the enemy's armed forces. "Loudspeaker and
leaflet units back up the Army's . . . operation, and exploit each

military success with a psychological pursuit aimed at fostering demoralization and desertion."[7]

3. To re-educate captured enemy personnel.

The duties of *guerre psychologique* obviously touched on most aspects of the war. Members of the 5es Bureaux shared in the planning of every type of operation, from an attack on an FLN strongpoint to the resettlement of a village, and assisted in carrying it out. Numerous missions were conceived by them and executed under their leadership. Equally, the scope of *action psychologique* was difficult to delimit. If the 5es Bureaux took literally the mission assigned to them of "assuring the cohesion of the whole of the nation and developing the will to fight in everyone," they could hardly keep from becoming actively involved in the political life of France.

Theories and Techniques

For the accomplishment of their military and nonmilitary tasks, the 5es Bureaux required, first, a satisfactory ideology, or, to put it differently, a social, political, and psychological program capable of eliciting general support in the nation. Further, they needed theories on the psychology of individuals and groups that would render possible the manipulation of people on a large scale, and the techniques and personnel to turn their ideas into reality. On the first point the psychological specialists failed. No truly effective ideology, it has already been suggested, emerged during the Algerian War; the conflicts of interests and motives among the adherents of *guerre révolutionnaire* were never more than superficially glossed over, and the doctrine's premises of a monolithic, authoritarian society were never accepted by a majority in the services and the country. The second requirement, the mobilization of psychological expertise against the FLN, was only partially fulfilled.[8]

The 5es Bureaux derived their ideas from a narrow body of psychological and sociological thought. Among Pavlovians, they found support for their belief that people could be conditioned to act and even to think in specific ways. Gustave Le Bon taught them that members of crowds tend to suppress their wishes and attitudes as individuals in favor of the will of the group, a will that could be created or at least manipulated by outside agencies. Most important, a Marxist follower of Pavlov, Serge Chakhotin (Tchakhotine), showed them how crude behavioral psychology could be combined with the techniques of commercial and political propaganda into a program for political action. In his book *The Rape of the Masses,* which was published a few months before the outbreak of World War II, Chakhotin analyzed the techniques of popular control employed by the European dictators, and argued that these methods should be turned against them.[9] Science, he claimed, had demonstrated that political action was "like all human action [primarily] a form of biological behavior" and that desirable actions—for example, the overthrow of Hitler—could be stimulated and brought about if the Western democracies would only use the proper techniques.[10]

> It will not suffice [he wrote] to prohibit the Nazi and Fascist movements, to persecute them by police measures. . . . There is only one effective method—to meet them with violent propaganda, to counteract their tendency to psychical rape by equivalent action on the psyche of the masses, but without recourse to lying. [Furthermore,] . . . it will not suffice to combat the Fascisms of today and annihilate them; it will be necessary to build up in men's mentality, in the functional structure of their mechanisms of behavior, reflexes which will render impossible a return to the state in which humanity is at present desperately struggling. The great ideas of Freedom, Peace, Love of all that is human, must become integral parts of our nature, reflexes anchored deeply in every human being.

This utopia Chakhotin proposed to achieve "by a judicious formation of appropriate conditioned reflexes, by propaganda, and above all by education"[11]—the latter, in his view, consisting of the constant reiteration of such concepts as "All men are equal," or "War is evil." If Chakhotin's arguments provided an attractive intellectual cloak to officers in search of a doctrine, it was undoubtedly his actual experiences as an antifascist propagandist in Germany and the lessons he had learned from such Nazi theorists as Eugen Hadamovsky that carried a more immediate message: Symbols, slogans, repetition, demonstrations, and violence—real as well as symbolic—could be used to forge a mass will, or, what amounted to the same, to keep the population regimented and docile. Over all loomed the experience of Indochina, notably the Vietminh efforts at re-educating French prisoners, which gave practical expression to the Communists' concept of the inadmissibility of ideological dissent as well as to their belief that a properly contrived environment can cure any human failing, including the possession of defective thoughts. But despite the work of a new group of Army-oriented "social psychologists," among whom the right-wing Catholic Georges Sauge became particularly influential, no effective synthesis of these ideas was achieved. In the end, the theorizing attempted by the 5es Bureaux and by their civilian allies amounted to little more than bids for support for an already chosen policy of complete human management and control.

The task at hand was, in any case, beyond the capacity of psychologists. To be useful, their theories not only had to explain how to manipulate a mass and re-educate an individual, but also had to ensure that the influence exerted was more than temporary. It has been argued that the demonstrations of French-Moslem friendship in May, 1958, were the greatest achievement of the 5es Bureaux. Certainly, they had an immediate political effect; in the long run, however, policy could not be based on theatrics in the Algiers Forum, but only on the day-to-day obedience of millions of individuals. How to prevent a brainwashed Moslem from backsliding into nationalism once he had been released from his re-education camp proved an insoluble problem. The Army psychol-

ogists could come up with no answer other than continuing as far
as possible on the outside the conditions of close control prevailing in the camps, of enmeshing the individual into networks of administrative, social, political, and economic hierarchies, by which
his behavior could be constantly checked and guided into the
proper channels. The belief that suitable psychological treatment
could bring about any desired reaction was thus linked, not surprisingly, to the concept of the authoritarian society.

The techniques of the 5es Bureaux ranged from means of mass
persuasion—propaganda companies, the press, so-called officers on
mission—to the intense re-education of individuals. The Army's
loudspeaker and pamphlet companies—*compagnies de hauts-par-
leurs et de tracts* (CHPT)—were a product of the North African
war.[12] The first three were established in September, 1956, and
attached to the three corps engaged in Algeria. The fourth company was raised in October of the following year and based in
Vincennes, on the outskirts of Paris, where, besides carrying out
missions among units stationed in metropolitan France, it served
as instruction center for propaganda personnel. The CHPT acted
under the direct authority of the 5e Bureau of the Army General
Staff. In make-up and duties, they resembled the Allied and German propaganda companies of World War II. They were
equipped with duplicating machines or printing presses, loud-
speakers, screens and projectors, a workshop to produce posters
and visual-training aids. To the French units, they presented
training films and programs on current affairs; to the Moslems,
they distributed leaflets, showed films, and broadcast music and
propaganda, usually in close conjunction with a military or police
operation. For example, during the March, 1957, campaign that
destroyed the FLN terrorist network in the Algiers area, the
CHPT distributed more than 2 million leaflets.[13]

A second group of specialists of the 5es Bureaux, the *officiers itinérants*—officers on mission—were sent into the field to back up or evaluate an operation from the point of view of psychological warfare, to explain the aims and methods of the 5es Bureaux to the local officers, and to give some elementary instruction in psychological action and psychological warfare to the troops. Their message was reinforced by a center for training in the concepts of *guerre révolutionnaire,* established by Colonel Lacheroy in Arzew, through which passed nearly all regular and reserve officers serving in Algeria.

Pertaining solely to *action psychologique* were the numerous official service publications, which continue to be published today, though their tone has altered somewhat since the military revolt of April, 1961. The widest circulation was enjoyed by the weekly *Bled,* which was distributed free to the services, and in 1959 had a regular run of at least 280,000 copies.[14] *Bled* was printed both in Paris and in Algiers and addressed itself specifically to the rank and file; at times, it followed a frankly authoritarian line. Of higher quality was the *Revue Militaire d'Information,* appearing monthly (occasionally every other month), with well-illustrated articles on defense problems and international affairs. Usually, 12,000 copies were printed, but for particularly important issues this figure was greatly exceeded.[15] The monthly *Revue de Défense Nationale* reflected the views of the General Staff and other top echelons. With its sober, authoritative manner, it was, and continues to be, somewhat reminiscent of *Foreign Affairs.* Further service publications included *Bellona, Cols-bleus, Kepi-blanc* (the journal of the Foreign Legion), *Notes et Documents, Revue des Forces Terrestres, Revue des Forces Aériennes, Revue Maritime, Soldat d'Outre-mer.* Finally, there were the *Messages d'Action Psychologique*—short position papers issued by the Ministry of National Defense on the government's views of national and international issues. The whole formed an impressive array of printed paper; but as the continuing distaste for revolutionary methods of the majority of the troops showed, the publications proved less effective in molding the opinions of their military public than in expressing the points of view of an increasingly isolated minority.

Reindoctrination Centers

The efforts of the psychological services to maintain French morale and to destroy the enemy's willingness to fight were almost wholly directed at the mass—radio and poster did not single out the individual from the group. The attempt to re-educate captured opponents, on the other hand, dealt largely with human beings in isolation. If the Algerian War was a conflict of ideologies, as the 5es Bureaux claimed, the conversion of the enemy constituted a mission of central importance. The winning of Moslem adherence could justify the French stand better than anything else, in their own eyes as well as in world opinion. Equally, nothing else could hurt FLN operations as severely or surpass the effect on the confidence of the rebel leaders. But the successful implementation of this mission presented difficulties. True conversion, the psychological specialists agreed, was achieved through prolonged treatment of the individual; how could this be carried out in a war of millions? The numbers involved—too many cases for conversion and too few practitioners—the inadequacy of psychological theories, and the skepticism of many soldiers and police about the superiority of persuasion over repression combined instead to tie the French reindoctrination program closely to the security measures taken to maintain control of the population.

In the early stages of the Algerian rebellion, FLN prisoners who escaped immediate execution generally were taken before French courts. As the fighting spread, it became apparent that the judicial process was too cumbersome to meet the conditions of civil war, and that it could adapt itself only with difficulty to the new concepts of *guerre psychologique* and *guerre révolutionnaire*. The

Army therefore established a system of processing prisoners that was almost entirely under its own control. The main components of this system, the internment camps, were illegal until Premier Guy Mollet was given special powers on March, 1956; but as early as July, 1955, a circular issued by Jacques Soustelle, then Governor General of Algeria, laid down regulations for the use of these camps. Two main types of camp were organized: the *centres de triage et de transit* (clearing and transit centers, CTT), and the *centres d'hébergement* (internment camps).[16] The CTT served as collecting points for suspects taken in police raids and military operations. The identities, loyalties, and involvement in the fighting of the detainees were to be determined within thirty days, after which they were placed in one of three groups:

1. The Reds, who were sent to trial.
2. The Whites, who were liberated "as quickly as possible."
3. The Pinks, against whom sufficiently grave evidence could not be established, "but who nevertheless remain dangerous."

The members of the third category were transferred to internment camps, where an attempt was made to reclaim as many as possible for the French cause.[17]

Officially, the system of the internment camps was controlled by a civilian prefect, but each camp was commanded by an officer, and he and his subordinates were generally selected by the 5es Bureaux. During the last years of the war, 10 such camps were acknowledged, with a total population of 8,000 inmates at any one time; the actual numbers of camps and prisoners were almost certainly far greater.[18] Assisting the Camp Commandant were the usual administrative and security personnel, as well as a psychological officer seconded by "psychological monitors," each of whom was placed in charge of a small group of prisoners. The prisoners themselves were reclassified as *durs* (hard), totally committed to the FLN; *moux* (soft), possible converts to the French cause; and *recoupérables* (curable), probable converts.

According to the official directive for "Psychological Action in the Internment Camps," the purpose of reindoctrination was to "reclaim for the Franco-Moslem community French citizens who are aware of France's will to remain in Algeria, and to institute reforms that are necessary to bring about peace and the happiness and prosperity of the Franco-Moslem community."[19] The reindoctrination process, the directive stated, "continues from morning to night. It is *led* by the Director of Psychological Action, *undertaken* by monitors who are helped by trustworthy prisoners (*hommes de confiance*), *controlled* by patient and minute observation of the prisoners' reactions." The first step in the process was to "disintegrate the individual." The internee was isolated, his fears and guilt feelings were exploited by his monitor, he was made to feel ashamed of his past and induced to acknowledge his errors. The period of brainwashing (*lavage de crâne*) was followed by a period of reconstruction or brainfilling (*bourrage de crâne*). Lectures and discussions presented the internee with the Army's views on history, current affairs, and the future of North Africa. In the final stage, the individual was brought into a disciplined group of converted fellow prisoners, which acted as an unfriendly collective superego toward recalcitrant inmates and which participated in the psychological campaign against the FLN beyond the barbed wire by writing propaganda letters to relatives and issuing manifestoes. Prisoners who attained this state of cooperation gained the right to participate in any paid work-program that the camp staff had been able to organize. According to the specialists of AP, the time needed to effect a conversion varied from six months for a fanatically anti-French private of the FLN to one and a half years for an NCO, and even longer for an officer. But, added the *Notice sur l'Action Psychologique,* since the number of truly fanatical is relatively small, "we may expect that 'recuperation' of individuals in the *centres d'hébergement* will demand very much shorter periods."

The measure of success these policies achieved is as difficult to establish precisely as it is to discover how many men were subjected to the reindoctrination process. A source very close to the 5es Bureaux claimed that of the inmates in the camp at Mazagran, all of whom were political or military officers of the rebellion, 50 per cent rallied to the French cause, 10 per cent rejoined the FLN, and 40 per cent remained neutral.[20] The basis for these figures is not given, but such favorable results seem wholly incompatible both with the outcome of the Algerian conflict and with the situations that prevailed in the camps.

The *centres d'hébergement* never had psychological monitors in adequate numbers to subject each inmate to that massive regimen of individual questioning that seems a prerequisite for successful brainwashing and re-education. Crude weekly crash programs stressing hygiene, patriotism, discipline, etc., and self-criticism meetings took their place; and it is difficult to believe that such directed mass-activities could produce any lasting effects in the prisoners' minds other than antagonism. The level of psychological sophistication among French personnel varied from camp to camp, as did the concern of the staff to re-educate the inmates rather than to punish them. Many camps lacked funds to institute sufficient work- and study-programs, so that the men had too much time to themselves. All this was conducive to the establishment of FLN networks in the camps, and even if an inmate could evade rebel control there, he would find it difficult to escape the power of the parallel hierarchies once he had been released.

Men who have spent three months in a CTT [wrote an officer in 1960] are afraid to return to their mountain homes, where an FLN cell rules and where they will again be drafted into the fight. . . . Without denying that they may feel some loyalty to the rebellion, it is clear to me that these men lack any degree of personal liberty whether they are subjected to the terror of the rebel organization or whether they sleep behind barbed wire. . . .[21]

The Algerian was caught in a crossfire, but of the two sources of danger—the French and the Nationalists—France in the long run proved the weaker. Despite its control of the machinery of government and administration, and despite its psychological-warfare armory, France was unable to match the diffused but continuous moral and physical pressure that a native, nationalistic revolutionary movement can exert on the people.

Atrocities

The *Notice sur l'Action Psychologique* cautioned that brutality by the camp guards was an error to be avoided at all costs in the re-education process. Yet brutality and torture were present in this stage of pacification as in all others. Officially, they formed no part of the doctrine of *guerre révolutionnaire,* but they belonged to its reality.

Atrocities are not unique to the Algerian conflict. They always occur when men fight, and civil wars with their special psychological stresses are particularly favorable to them. What differentiated the situation that developed in Algeria from somewhat similar cases, such as the Malayan emergency and the campaign against the EOKA in Cyprus, was both its greater incidence of torture and brutality and its greater degree of institutionalization.

Reliable evidence on this matter is hard to come by. The accusations of the FLN must be suspect, as are those of any interested party. Often they were pure propaganda, expressing horror at alleged French actions while keeping silent about rebel terror campaigns against Algerians and Europeans. Under prevailing conditions, even many of their plausible claims have been impossible to verify. But the Nationalists and their occasional propaganda allies, the Communists, are not the only sources available. For years, Frenchmen and foreigners, soldiers, government officials, and civilians, with political views ranging from right-wing authoritarianism to that of the extreme left, have testified to the kinds and frequency of the torture and terror practiced on Algerians in the name of France. The trials of OAS members during the summer of 1962 produced further evidence. Right-wing sympathizers found it easier to give such testimony since atrocities were not the preserve of one particular party or ideology, socialist ministers and officials being involved as well as moderates and conservatives of many hues.

This is not the place to give even a summary history of the atrocities committed on the French side during the seven years of fighting. The state of affairs that existed during the later years of the war may, however, be suggested by citing a few statements of individuals and organizations that can be suspected neither of Communism nor of being sympathetic to the rebel cause. In his press conference of June 24, 1958, shortly after General de Gaulle's assumption of power, André Malraux admitted that French forces had tortured Algerians. The government's Commission for Safeguarding Individual Rights and Liberties reported that it had found incontrovertible evidence of torture and of French disregard of the laws of war. Early in 1959, the Army's Catholic Chaplains' Office issued a document entitled *Study of Moral Behavior in a Subversive War,* which characterized torture of Algerians as being of questionable military value and inherently wicked and corrupting.[22] In March of the same year, a unanimous report signed by thirty-five priests who had served as reserve officers in Algeria appealed to their bishops for guidance in the moral dilemmas created by the practices of some French authorities in Algeria.

> From a comparison of our experiences, it emerges broadly that methods are used in the conduct of war that our consciences condemn. Arbitrary arrests and detentions are numerous. Interrogations are conducted only too generally by methods that we must call torture.

Summary executions of prisoners, both civilian and military, ordered by judicial authorities, but concealed on the plea of "attempted flight" and given cover by official reports, are not exceptional. Finally, it is not unusual during operations for the wounded to be finished off. We must add that these practices extend down to the smallest unit of military organization.

Their painstakingly objective report continues:

To this account of the facts, we must add these qualifications:

a. In certain regions, directives contrary to this trend have been given by military authorities. Even when these orders are not applied or are poorly applied, it is important to note them. To our knowledge, punishments have been enforced against certain officers responsible for this state of affairs.

b. While we say these practices are very widespread, we insist that they are not universal. They do not apply in sectors that are militarily quiet. Further, we have all known, even in the most disturbed areas, officers or men of remarkable character who have succeeded in creating about them a state of mind contrary to such practices.

c. Finally, as officers serving in Algeria, we can say that this state of affairs is not only or primarily the Army's responsibility. But the non-recognition of a state of war and the almost total lack of a suitable judicial organization often make it in practice impossible for the military authorities to carry out their tasks within the limits of legality and morality.[23]

Similar criticism of the arrangements for trying suspected supporters of the Nationalist cause had already been voiced in the report of the Army's Catholic Chaplains' Office, which urged the military authorities to demand "the establishment at the earliest possible moment of a judicial system conforming to the needs of the Algerian situation." After De Gaulle's assumption of power, the well-entrenched opposition to judicial reform was slowly beaten down. During the first year of the Fifth Republic, the number of military tribunals increased from three to twelve, making possible a more orderly process of law. The Court of Appeals, until then sitting in Algeria, now moved to the somewhat calmer atmosphere of Paris. These were improvements within the old system. In November, 1959, a commission of soldiers and jurists was established to study the possibilities of basic reform. The commission submitted its recommendations on January 14, 1960, only a few days before the recall of General Massu precipitated the "Week of the Barricades," and they were acted upon in the wave of reorganization that followed the abortive insurrection. From this time on, civilian judges presided over the military tribunals, courts were attached to the lower military echelons, and the whole legal process was speeded up. The two main objectives of these and other reforms were to reassert civilian control over justice and to get the prisoners as quickly as possible out of the hands of the units that had captured them, since investigations showed that most brutalities occurred at this early stage.

It proved more difficult to influence the situation in the camps and military prisons. These did not fall under the jurisdiction of the Ministry of Justice, but were considered an internal service responsibility, with the camp commandants and sector or district commanders possessing considerable autonomy.[24] Conditions varied greatly. Of the forty-three *centres de triage et de transit* that the International Red Cross visited between October 15 and November 27, 1959, it judged more than half in the Constantine and Oran areas to be efficiently and humanely run.[25] In the Algiers sector, however, the delegation found conditions satisfactory in less than a third of the camps and frankly bad in over a third. One colonel in charge of a camp on the outskirts of Algiers admitted the use of torture on detainees, and claimed that "the fight against terrorism makes certain methods of interrogation indispensable as the only way to save human lives and avoid new attacks." In numerous camps, prisoners complained of having been subjected to beatings and torture by electricity and water, accounts that the physician accompanying the delegation could frequently substantiate. In one camp, the visitors entered a cell that contained 6 men, 3 of whom showed evidence of recent beatings, and a corpse. In another camp, 580 men were crowded into quarters for 300, had been issued neither blankets nor mattresses, and were subjected to such severe treatment that they had become "completely terrorized."

> [Previous visits by Red Cross representatives, stated the report,] conversations with the officers responsible, and their negative attitude, confirm the impression that theirs was a deliberate position and that any request for improvement was useless. We cannot avoid thinking that the miserable conditions of this camp are intended, and form part of a system. Though this attitude may secure some results in the short run (the intelligence service claims to have obtained important results), it is inhuman, and in flagrant contradiction with the most elementary humanitarian principles.

Finally an appeal to General Challe, then Commander in Chief in Algeria, led to improvements. When Red Cross delegates revisited the camp some weeks later, more than 200 inmates had been transferred, and brutalities during interrogation had ceased. Other camps proved less susceptible to outside pressure. In the summer of 1960, the League of the Rights of Man, at its Forty-eighth Congress, issued a unanimous report, declaring that torture still "continues to exist in Algeria, that it dishonors the French Army, our Flag, and our values, which we intend to defend."[26] The fight against the FLN proved in fact inseparable from the mistreatment of Algerians, and even the new regime, with its pronounced desire for reform, could not wholly uproot practices that had acquired the authority of custom.[27]

Aside from a rare admission by a soldier or official, it remained the policy of the government as well as of the services to deny that brutality or torture were more than exceptional occurrences. Public discussion of the subject was generally interpreted as an attempt to sabotage the war in Algeria. "Unfriendly propaganda,"

Captain Souyris wrote as early as 1957, "can find isolated instances [of torture], which in no way correspond to official directives and are severely punished."[28] In their defense of French methods, however, official spokesmen frequently compromised their own case. Characteristic was an editorial in the Army publication *Bled* that pointed out that both the government and the High Command expressly condemned torture, and continued, "What is the truth behind this word? People try to make it mean everything . . . simple physical and mental coercion, secret interrogations, blows and ill-treatment: People say 'torture' instead of 'brutality' and thus change excesses into crime."[29] Privately, even adherents of the doctrine of *guerre révolutionnaire* would admit that the maltreatment of prisoners and the use of torture to gain information was normal in some commands, and that even if such treatment were not rendered necessary by the nature of the Algerian conflict, it was impossible to control the actions of every Army or *gendarmerie* unit. Here as elsewhere, weakness of the central authority clearly posed serious problems; but there is also strong evidence to suggest that at times specific orders to employ torture were issued by—or with the knowledge of—senior officials and officers. That torture was used generally rather than as an exception during such operations as the Battle of Algiers has been stated repeatedly by officers who took part in the actions. During a recent trial of three OAS terrorists, for example, a former Captain of the 1st Parachute Regiment of the Foreign Legion, appearing as character witness for one of the accused, stated:

[He] like a hundred other officers received at this time [January, 1957] the order to torture with a view to collecting information. I do not know which was the high authority that originally gave this order. You will never see it in writing. I only know that for the 10th Parachute Division, it was General Massu who transmitted it. Without him, how could it have happened that on a certain day of January, 1957, the four regiments of his division set about collecting information? The operation had a name: it was "Opération Champagne." Don't ask me for details. I don't know what hell the man went through who gave the order. But I know the rape it was for the young men straight from St. Cyr. All myths and illusions crashed together. They were told that the end justifies the means, and that France's victory depended on it.[30]

Collecting additional evidence on the extent to which torture played a part in the Algerian War is by now less important than inquiring into the reasons for its use. Certainly much maltreatment was due to individuals acting on their own initiative, for their own purposes. Numerous other cases were clearly the responsibility of men in positions of authority, who could be expected to see beyond the limits of their command and consider the effects such illegal acts might have on the Army, the nation, and the country's relations with other states.[31] Since the impact in these areas was great and wholly unfavorable, it must be assumed that their motives for employing torture were particularly weighty ones. When an explanation for their actions was offered at all, it was generally that torture was a useful means to gain information. This belief, widely held throughout the world, was based on considerable experience, though it ignored the possibility that foreknowledge of harsh treatment might repel potential sources of information. Equally, little was ever said about the different kinds of information sought. Maltreatment was the easiest to defend and condone in the acquisition of tactical intelligence, which needed to be obtained as quickly as possible, since even slight delays could render it useless. Information of a political nature, on the organization of the rebel network, for example, did not become dated at once and could be gained more reliably through interrogation and analysis of other sources. Finally, a prisoner's admission that he supported the rebels or sympathized with their cause could only rarely possess operational significance; torturing a prisoner to obtain such a confession could not be explained by the need to prevent an ambush or terrorist attack.

The brutal treatment of prisoners, whether they had been newly captured or held for months, was often motivated by considerations that had nothing to do with intelligence-gathering. Algerians were tortured in reprisal for FLN actions, as a means of terrorizing the rebel cadres and the population.[32] Reprisal and terror could be considered rationally as weapons in an intense struggle between ideologically opposed and necessarily ruthless opponents; but it was hardly possible to keep conception and execution of such actions on a detached plane. Personal emotions, hatred and sadism, could not help but play a determining part in the torture of prisoners, regardless of how convincingly this was presented as an essential operational device, and this fact possessed general as well as private significance. Government and Army felt themselves compelled to throw the cloak of authority over the ambiguous motives of individuals, and one more item was added to the troublesome list of inconsistencies and dishonesties in their Algerian policies.

Using torture, even to gain important tactical information, carried with it further serious implications. Too many officers and men were unable to reconcile their participation in brutalities—or even their knowledge of them—with their moral beliefs. The resultant bad conscience and guilt feelings, which psychological-warfare officers vainly ridiculed in their indoctrination courses, the loss of respect for superiors, the profound division of opinion on the matter, had a powerful impact on the Army's discipline and morale. Traditional-minded soldiers refused to acknowledge the need for torture in any circumstance. General Pierre Billotte wrote:

On the subject of torture, I am unequivocal: in whatever form, for whatever purpose, it is unacceptable, inadmissible, to be condemned; it casts a slur on the honor of Army and country. The ideological character of modern war changes nothing in this. On the contrary, in struggles of this kind, victory eventually falls to the more noble ideology; the greater respect for moral and human values constitutes one of the most effective means of gaining victory since it goes directly to the hearts of men who are temporarily hostile. Besides, the excuse heard occasionally that one tortured man may perhaps save a hundred of our own is not valid. First, in very few instances does the unfortunate prisoner possess information of such importance. Furthermore and above all, though this is a cruel duty, a commanding officer must not hesitate to expose his men and even the population under his protection to greater danger rather than make use of a dishonorable practice. A commander who lacks the moral strength to carry out such a duty does not deserve to command French troops. The spirit of sacrifice is the cardinal virtue of the soldier.[88]

Revolutionary war may have outdated this high regard for honor and sacrifice, but the point that decent behavior would go further than repression in winning popular support is timeless common sense. If, however, gaining support of the population was not the relevant objective, this consideration would not apply; the efficacy of terror for immobilizing active opposition among a hostile people can hardly be doubted. General Billotte's arguments had the additional advantage of agreeing with the generally accepted moral tenets of French society, thus being unifying in import rather than divisive. As might be expected, the service chaplains and the great majority of the Catholic and Protestant clergy joined in totally rejecting torture. A characteristic statement by a parish priest declared that on this issue

all France ought to be in agreement, from the extreme right to the extreme left. Even if it was only because of the inevitable abuses, torture is inadmissible, even if it is a matter of obtaining information from an admittedly guilty man. One can only despise the cowardly individuals who practice, order, or tolerate such horrors. . . . Christians ought long ago to have raised their voice in protest without worrying with what other voices it would be mingled, or scrutinizing the intentions of other protests. . . . We are responsible as Frenchmen for the tortures whose employment is spreading like gangrene. It is the very archetype of collective sin. We are all torturers if by a collusive silence we allow it to happen. Don't tell me that a diplomatic action undertaken in secret is more effective than a public protest. Six years have proved the contrary.[34]

Hurting the innocent was one of the "inevitable abuses" connected with torture. Another, and one of more immediate concern to the services, was the process of degradation that caught up the soldiers who administered the beatings and the water- and electrical-treatments, and passed from them to the rest of the Army. Charging small groups of specialists with these duties might have provided some measure of control, but the number of victims actually involved and their wide geographic dispersion made secrecy impossible. And even if only specialists had been implicated, which was not the case, knowledge of their activities was bound to spread to the regular units who carried out the necessary security, transport, and supply duties, and from them to the Army as a whole.[35] Only commanders who were indifferent to the prevailing moral standards, or who actively opposed them, would have willingly run the risk of infecting society with the lack of respect for the individual that is inherent in systematic physical and psychological brutality.

Those who believed that people should be manipulated to act and react in certain definite ways found it easy to accept physical violence as an instrument in the conditioning process. The warning against brutality expressed in the *Notice sur l'Action Psychologique* did nothing to dispel this attitude, which was powerfully reinforced by the view that the Algerian War formed part of a universal ideological struggle, in which the nonbeliever had to be converted, punished, or killed. As a result, men who claimed to defend Western society against the godless employed methods that compromised the values they sought to uphold, and did so without being faced by the immediate overwhelming crisis that alone might have justified their acts.

As an escape from this dilemma, the suggestion was sometimes put forward that the ruthlessness of the FLN made torture not only necessary but excusable. Psychological-warfare officers argued that, after all, an essential difference existed between the aim of the French operations and those of their opponents, and that this difference made the similarity of their methods unimportant. Form and content of psychological warfare—"*le contenant et le contenu*"—were said to be distinct and not to be confused.[36] But although it could be argued that publicity campaigns as such are morally neutral, and that all depends on their message, this hardly applies to a program of extreme physical coercion. The attempt to draw such a parallel did, however, indicate the extent to which totalitarian concepts had become accepted in the 5es Bureaux.

In North Africa, the physical excesses that are always met with in war were reinforced by ideological considerations which not only failed to restrain brutality and ruthlessness, but, on the contrary, fostered and institutionalized them. The price paid—whether consciously understood or not—was dissension in the armed forces and in society and a serious weakening of the country's international position. So far as the war itself went, torture and the unavoidable knowledge of it made a farce of pacification. In the end, the recourse to such methods was an admission of defeat: Atrocities made re-education in a nontotalitarian sense impossible.

The Breakup of the 5es Bureaux

Between 1957 and the settlers' insurrection of January, 1960, the 5es Bureaux were almost entirely free of control from Paris. They could develop their own methods of psychological action and psychological warfare, they were also able to assume a growing share in the formulation of the ideology and the political program these methods were to advance. From a subordinate agency of the government and the armed forces, *action psychologique* changed into a policy-making body whose members showed increasing readiness to interpret and even adapt policy to suit their view of the operational requirements in Algeria. Since they held that the clash between revolution and counterrevolution demanded total unity of the counterrevolutionary base and its armed forces, they extended their activities to metropolitan France: Not only were the services to be trained to fight a revolutionary war, but French society itself had to be cleansed and reoriented.

The indoctrination of the services seemed easier to achieve immediately than the regeneration of France. Officers and men could be subjected to intensive education and propaganda courses without running the risk of anything more serious than an occasional individual protest. The strong political and financial backing the 5es Bureaux received from the Algerian ultras and from such government officials as Jacques Soustelle facilitated their expansion within the Army and enabled them to acquire responsibilities that were far removed from their original mission. They supervised resettlement of the population, ran the program that attempted to create a corps of pro-French Moslem administrators, directed the work of the welfare and medical teams and of the youth-guidance personnel. But their accumulation of power stimulated opposition. Senior officers as well as units in the field, an observer noted at the beginning of 1960, were showing considerable hostility toward the staffs of the 5es Bureaux, who frequently assumed the roles of personal confidants of the High Command or of political commissars. In December, 1959, the government made its first serious attempt to halt the encroachment by transferring some of the most radical officers, such as Colonel Gardes, Chief of the 5e Bureau in Algiers, to less sensitive duties, and placing ultimate responsibility for psychological action in the hands of a three-man commission under the Delegate General and the Commander in Chief in Algeria. These reforms, which appear to have been in the nature of a probe, were almost at once overtaken by events.

Their concern with French indifference or opposition to the Algerian War pushed the 5es Bureaux deeply into politics. In time, their position came to approximate closely that of the activist elements among the French settlers and of the neofascists in metropolitan France. Officers of the 5es Bureaux helped organize and indoctrinate *colons* into political shock troops that could be used to pressure the government. By 1959, they openly boasted of controlling these movements, adding that as their members were civilians or reservists, their rowdyism and worse could not be charged to the Army. Such statements, as well as the evidence that was brought out in subsequent trials, make it apparent that the government's effort in December, 1959, to circumscribe the power of the 5es Bureaux was a factor in triggering the riots of the Algiers mob the following month. Paris did not fail to draw the obvious conclusion. In February, after order had been re-established, Colonel Gardes was arrested for inciting rebellion, and the 5es Bureaux were abolished. Their duties were divided between the 2nd and 3rd Sections of the General Staff, an interservice coordinating body, and the Study and Liaison Bureau of the Combined General Staff (Bureau d'Études et Liaison de l'État-Major Interarmées). Their information and propaganda functions were further shared with a new agency, the Centre d'Information Générale, which was placed under the authority of the Delegate General, the civilian head of French administration in Algeria.[37]

The breakup of the 5es Bureaux was an important step in the process of drawing the Army out of politics. But although the special units had disappeared, their mission and their methods remained. The program of psychological action, which had so strongly influenced military operations in Algeria, could not be scrapped overnight, nor could the civil authorities—themselves divided and lacking a clear lead from Paris—immediately lay down new guidelines for propaganda and political warfare. In principle, the Army had been forced to relinquish some of its most important nonmilitary duties; in reality, however, it continued to be responsible for their implementation—if only because in many cases an alternative could not be found. Few civilian doctors, for example, were willing to take over the ill-paid and dangerous jobs of the SAS medical teams. Once again, the Army was faced with the dilemma of how to fight a war in which success was greatly dependent on nonmilitary action, whose adequate performance in turn required a degree of social and economic mobilization that the government felt unable to impose. For the psychological-warfare officers, the issue was not resolved until 1961, when most accepted De Gaulle's decision to negotiate with the FLN and withdraw from Algeria. Some, however, refused to obey. The generals' revolt in May was largely engineered by veterans of the 5es Bureaux, who subsequently played leading roles in the OAS effort to retain Algeria by terror. That neither the Army nor the nation joined them in insurrection was final proof that their missionary efforts were as ineffective among Frenchmen as they had been among the FLN and the Moslem population. On balance, despite all their efforts, the achievement of the 5es Bureaux was poor. Fighting a colonial war in mid-twentieth century posed grave problems to a democracy and to its propaganda services. This had not gone unrecognized; but the recourse by the 5es Bureaux to totalitarian concepts and methods, which were neither backed by sufficient physical force nor generally accepted by the nation, proved a costly and dangerous dead end.

Chapter 6

The Doctrine in Action: Opération Pilote

How did the different components of the French answer to revolutionary warfare work together in practice? What could theory, organization, and training achieve operationally? The following report may serve to illustrate their interaction in the field. It is an account, written by Colonel Cazelles, the officer in charge, of a politico-military operation executed during 1957 and 1958 in a small coastal area of Algeria, east of Oran. As its code name indicates, the operation was an experiment.

OPÉRATION PILOTE[1]

It seems opportune to bring together in this report the results and the lessons of Opération Pilote, which was carried out in the Dahra of Oran this past year. This is done not to mark the anniversary of the operation's beginning, but because the results achieved in certain sections of the area now permit us to risk reducing the density of troops there and to proceed to the final phase of the operation.

I. *General Plan of Opération Pilote in the Dahra Mountains of Oran*

The objective of this particular Opération Pilote[a] was "to set up a Moslem politico-administrative superstructure that would enjoy the confidence of the people and be favorable to France."[b]

The area chosen for the operation was the Dahra Mountains of Oran, a part of the department of Mostaganem located north of the Chéliff River.

This area (henceforth called the "Pilot Area") was selected:

Because it forms a reasonably distinct whole within the Department of Mostaganem; and

Because, being a continuation of the Dahra of Algiers, it would permit expanding the area of Opération Pilote already launched in the Department of Orléansville.

The Pilot Area covers about 1,700 square kilometers [650 square miles]. It may be schematically divided into two roughly equal parts, separated by a string of peaks stretching from west to east, which begins at the mouth of the Chéliff River and is paralleled by the Bosquet–Cassaigne–Renault highway.

The coastal range consists of a series of fertile plateaus (chiefly vineyards), separated by embanked *oueds*. The southern side, drier and infertile, is made up of a series of ravines converging on the Chéliff; that are separated by small peaks (altitude under 800 meters [2,600 feet]), which are, however, steep and rugged. Roads and paths are infrequent and poor.

Out of a total population of about 120,000, the 3,000 who are of European stock live almost entirely in the urban centers of the northern side. The Moslem population, of Berber origin, is completely Arab in its ways.[c] Rugged by nature, these people submitted to French rule only after the strict repressive measures instituted by General Pélissier in 1847.

---

[a] A first Opération Pilote had been previously launched in the Department of Orléansville to provide experience for subsequent campaigns.

[b] Directive No. 1687/5 D.B./3.S of May 21, 1957.

[c] Worthy of note is the religious center of Mazouna (mentioned by [the fourteenth-century historian] Ibn Khaldoun) on the eastern boundary of the Department of Orléansville.

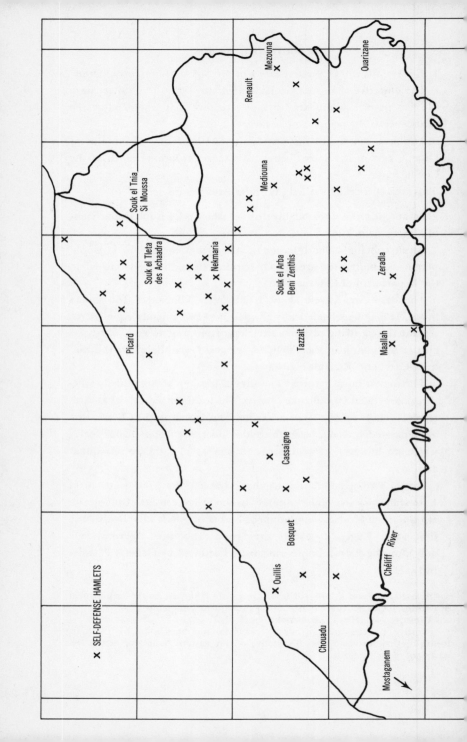

SELF-DEFENSE HAMLETS

Mostaganem

Chouadu

Chéliff River

Ouillis

Bosquet

Cassaigne

Picard

Souk el Tleta des Achaadra

Nekmaria

Souk el Tnia Si Moussa

Souk el Arba Beni Zenthis

Tazzait

Mediouna

Renault

Mezouna

Ouarizane

Maallah

Zeradla

Since that date, except for an outbreak at Renault at the time of the October, 1945, elections, there were relatively few incidents in the Dahra of Oran until November, 1954, when an attempted revolt in the neighborhood of Cassaigne was quickly put down.

Unrest broke out again in August and September, 1956 (including a new incident at Cassaigne). When the 5th Armored Division arrived in the Department of Mostaganem in March, 1957, the rebel political and administrative infrastructure was effective throughout the entire Oranian Dahra, and organized bands of from 100 to 200 men traversed the countryside.

On March 22, 1957, what was to become the Pilot Area was placed under the control of the colonel commanding the 5th Cavalry Brigade. From his two regiments he assigned to the area:[d]

the 6th Motorized Cavalry, half of which arrived on March 19, 1957, the other half on April 7.

the 1st Cuirassiers, who arrived on April 10. These were reinforced by an Armored Squadron of the 2nd Motorized Cavalry and the 31st Mobile Security Group from Cassaigne.

The 5th Cavalry Brigade simultaneously launched operations against the rebel infrastructure and the armed bands. The latter phase was quickly highlighted by two successes (northwest of Mediouna on March 26, and in the valley of the Kramis on May 28), which showed the bands that the forces of order had regained the initiative. Within three months, the activities of the 5th Cavalry Brigade had sufficiently weakened rebel influence to lead us to believe that a special psychological-warfare effort would bring useful results.

The chronology of the psychological-warfare effort on Opération Pilote may be divided into three phases:

1. From July to the end of December, 1957, which included: special training of units, first operations of psychological action.

2. From January to March, 1958: period of maximum effort.

3. As of March, 1958, a progressive reduction of military forces; at first necessitated by circumstances, later continued voluntarily because the operation was succeeding.

[d] Infantry regiments, each the size of a reinforced battalion.

II. *Means*

The means placed at the disposal of the Commander of the 5th Brigade to accomplish his mission were:

Additional units.

Resources of psychological action (personnel, matériel).

Funds spent in conjunction with the Civil Authority, which, for its part, speeded up the establishment of the SAS teams in the Pilot Area.

1. *Additional Units.* Failing to obtain the reinforcements requested, the General commanding the 5th Armored Division had to draw from his own zone of responsibility the forces he considered essential for the Pilot Area:

From the end of July to the end of December, 1957, 1 battalion and 1 battery.

From January to mid-March, 1958, 1 additional battalion and the 1st Composite Airborne Commando Group.

Subsequent transfers reduced these forces. After the end of March, 1958, reinforcements totaled only: 1 battalion of Algerian Skirmishers, 2 companies of "Nomads" [counterguerrilla companies], 1 artillery battery.[e]

It should be stressed that the reinforcements consisted almost wholly of Moslem troops, whose use in such proportions was not a priori desirable for this operation. Necessity, however, left no alternative.

2. *Resources of Psychological Action.* Between May, 1957, and April, 1958, the Pilot Area benefited greatly from the services of two mobile teams of officers.[f]

The 2nd Loudspeaker and Pamphlet Company was placed at the disposal of the Commanding Officer—at first partially (2 sections) from July to November, 1957, then *in toto* from November, 1957, to July, 1958. When the 2nd Company left, 5 loudspeaker teams without personnel were detached to the units of the 5th Cavalry Brigade.

Seven teams of Youth Counselors were brought to the Pilot Area (5 at the end of December, 1957, 2 at the end of May, 1958).

[e] *Note:* A company of engineers left the area in April, 1958; approximately 100 square kilometers [40 square miles] of the Sector of Tenes were added to the operational responsibility of the Commander of the sector.

[f] Captain Richard and Lieutenant Laine in May and June, 1957; Commander Guidon and Captain Berault until April, 1958. Since that time, Captain Berault has been alone on the job in that sector.

Some ASSRA [Assistantes Sociales Sanitaires Rurales de l'Algérie] and locally recruited auxiliary units (9 including 4 Moslem groups) were placed at the disposal of the local commands. In particular, they joined the medico-social teams, each led by a military doctor of the sector, for whose use 2 trucks of the 5th Armored Division were loaned by the 85th Quartermasters.

3. *Funds.* Special funds were placed at the disposal of the Prefect of Mostaganem (100 million francs to date). Paid without having to go through channels, at the joint request of the Sub–prefect and the District Commander, these funds permitted:

The purchase of articles necessary to the propaganda effort (signs, posters, photographic supplies, Assistance Médicale Gratuite matériel, etc.).

The distribution of relief, in cash or in kind.

Above all, the launching of work projects, which proved indispensable in gaining access to the douars (building of roads), or in improving the living conditions of the population (construction of housing, clinics), or in enabling the people to defend themselves (organization of the self-defense program). The funds made it possible to speed up projects that were already foreseen in the normal aid programs, and to bring these programs to completion.

4. *SAS.* At the request of the Commanding General, the Prefect of Mostaganem sought priority for the establishment of SAS teams in the Pilot Area.

To the 3 SAS teams existing in March, 1957, 2 more were added in May; 1 in June; 1 in September; 1 in November; and a final 1 in June, 1958.

III. *Method Adopted*

First of all, the rebel political and administrative network had to be destroyed. The units accomplished this destruction after their arrival in the zone of operations, while at the same time pursuing the armed bands—without giving priority to one or the other side of this coordinated effort.

Operations were facilitated by a knowledge of the inhabitants, which the 5th Cavalry Brigade made sure to acquire quickly, learning from its previous experiences in the sector of Nedroma. Identity papers, whose usefulness was apparent, were issued.[g]

On the constructive side—the setting up of a pro-French infrastructure—it had been intended in imitation of the methods adopted for the Opération Pilote of Orléansville, i.e., to install native cadres that had been surreptitiously selected, taken away, and trained.[h] At the same time, the creation of groups of armed auxiliaries would succeed in bolstering the "existing operational system."[i]

Experience led to a modification of these methods: The number of "secret cadres" that had been formed was not sufficient for us to hope that through them the pro-French political and administrative network would be appreciably strengthened. Though certainly useful, these men have served mainly as intelligence agents, working under dangerous conditions, and as "catalysts" speeding up the [pro-French] evolution of their districts.

We were, therefore, led to use former internees of "transit camps," who had been "re-educated" ["retournés"] by intense psychological treatment. Since the Commanding General of the 5th Armored Division lacked the means to conduct re-education programs in all camps, he created, in September, 1957, a special camp, Camp F, where groups of 20 to 30 trainees were "graduated" every other month.

Released at the same time as internees of other camps (though, like all released internees, a priori suspect to the FLN), they were sent back to their districts and entrusted to a responsible officer (a counter-intelligence officer or Commander of a subdistrict).[j]

---

[g] Cards, with a photograph of the individual, of which duplicates were kept in the subdistrict office and by the SAS teams. Without being regular *cartes d'identité*, these documents permit the authorities to keep an eye on everyone and to spot the arrival of strangers. The cards were first issued to the male population between the ages of eighteen and sixty. On September 15, 1957, that is, after five to six months, almost 24,000 cards existed—meaning that 80–90 per cent of the population group affected was signed up. At present, the same kind of operation is under way for the female population.

[h] Directive 1.687/5th D.B./3/S of May 21, 1957.

[i] Memorandum 7 attached to the same directive.

[j] Out of 250 trainees who completed the instruction period (more than half of whom were trained with the Pilot Area in view), one-third can be classified as Very Good or Good; one-third as Useful; one-third as Useless or Unfortunate Cases.

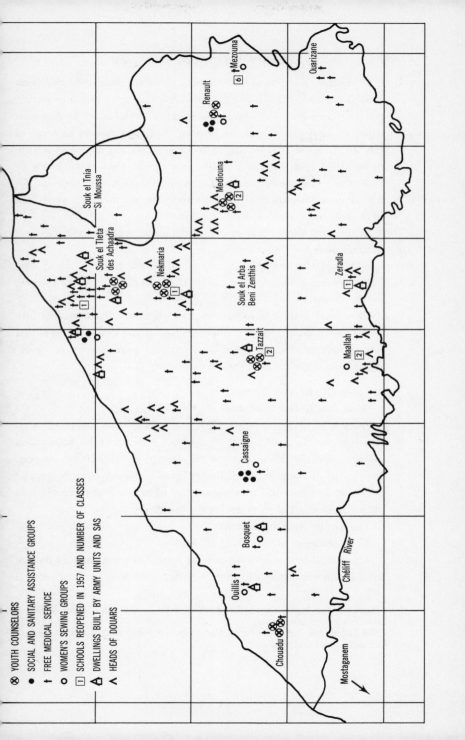

Legend:

⊗ YOUTH COUNSELORS

● SOCIAL AND SANITARY ASSISTANCE GROUPS

† FREE MEDICAL SERVICE

○ WOMEN'S SEWING GROUPS

1 SCHOOLS REOPENED IN 1957 AND NUMBER OF CLASSES

⌂ DWELLINGS BUILT BY ARMY UNITS AND SAS

∧ HEADS OF DOUARS

Mostaganem

Chéliff River

Chouadu

Ouilis

Bosquet

Cassaigne

Tazzait

Maallah

Zeradla

Souk el Arba
Beni Zenthis

Nekmaria

Souk el Tleta
des Achaadra

Souk el Tnia
Si Moussa

Mediouna

Renault

Mezouna

Ouarizane

Using these men, as well as friendly elements their units had been able to uncover, the District Commanders sought to put into power, working in cooperation with the SAS teams, a chief aided by 2 or 3 assistants.ᵏ To increase their usefulness, the Commanding General of the 5th Armored Division organized an orientation course at Rivoli, in mid-July, 1958. Attended by 40 douar chiefs or assistants chosen by SAS officers and the Subdistrict Commanders, the course provided fifteen days of basic training in civics and gave the members some idea of the roles they were expected to play.

At the same time, the District Commanders sought to increase their military potential:

By completing the defense and guard system through the arming (with hunting rifles) of those douars that had given proof of rallying [to the French cause].

By bolstering their units with harkas, some actually integrated into the units, others in groups of about 20 men living in douars organized for self-defense, and given missions (patrols, participation in operations) beyond the limits of their douars.

IV. *Results*

What results were achieved?

From July, 1957, to August, 1958, the action against the rebel infrastructure and the armed bands in the Pilot Area led to the inactivation of more than 70 rebels and the recovery of more than 20 weapons (two-thirds of them hunting pieces) by *each Battalion each month.*[1] We must also note the winning over of 63 rebels (one-third of them armed), almost all of them during the last three months.

The constructive side includes:

The enlistment of more than 400 harkas.

The establishment of a self-defense system in more than 50 douars, armed with more than 450 hunting rifles. The program concentrated

---

ᵏ This was the beginning of the effort to organize the population, which is presently nearing completion.

[1] 970 killed and 2,099 imprisoned and arrested; 897 weapons recovered, of which 607 were hunting pieces.

on the eastern section of the area in order to form a network of self-defending douars against the inroads of rebels coming from the Algerian Dahra. The trustworthiness of the native elements is illustrated by the simple facts that only 2 hunting rifles were lost through desertion[m] out of the nearly 900 weapons distributed—and that on several occasions (the last occurring between dusk of September 24 and dawn of September 25), self-defending douars repulsed rebel elements that had come to feel them out.

The putting into office of almost 60 douar chiefs trained at Rivoli, and of approximately 70 trainees of the re-education camp.[n]

The development of social services in their most varied forms.

A considerable increase in treatments given by the Assistance Médicale Gratuite (more than 150,000 consultations took place in the Pilot Area from June, 1957 to August, 1958).

The organization of needlework schools, of women's social groups; the opening or reopening of schools; building activity (clinics, dwellings); the organizing of sports activities by the Youth Counselors.

The expansion of the communications network by the construction of *"chemins de pacification"* and other roadways.

V. *Lessons*

In general, therefore, the experiment may be said to have been at least encouraging, if not conclusive.

It is encouraging both in view of the results outlined above and in view of the atmosphere now existing in that part of the area where self-defending douars are sufficiently numerous. This atmosphere can be attested to by any visitor, and is further revealed by the amount of information the population furnishes.

The experiment will be conclusive when, after the establishment of a sufficiently close-knit pattern of self-defending douars throughout

[m] In addition, 3 rifles were stolen by the rebels. The desertions occurred in April, 1958, on the very night following the arming of the douar. Since then, the self-defending elements and the harkas of this douar have, to a great extent, wiped this stain from their record.

[n] Note that a considerable number of other trainees, no longer useful as agents, had to discontinue this activity.

the whole Pilot Area,° we will be able progressively to withdraw our troops—a move presently in its early stages—without the loyalty of the population wavering.

It is not premature to draw some lessons from the operation:

1. The policy of a self-defense system of douars proved worthwhile.

It should be carried out cautiously, taking only calculated risks. As a general rule, it may be laid down that a self-defending douar should be no more than half an hour from an intervening military force. This has resulted: in occasionally detaching 1 platoon to the area of self-defending douars; and in multiplying the roads, to benefit from the possibilities of motorized transportation.

This explains the great effort spent on improving the communications network. It is therefore possible to state once more—it seems absurd to rediscover this after Lyautey—that the opening of a road created *ipso facto* significant progress in pacification.

It must be stressed that, in making the douars self-defending, we did not regroup, but often "centralized" the population: That is, to avoid transplanting the population more than one-half to three-quarters of an hour's walk from its normal places of work, and to avoid creating the problem of "displaced persons," we brought together, for reasons of security and facility in defense, the most distant dwellings into two or three groups of houses in each douar.

The solution of centralization has the advantage of not leaving terrain unoccupied that would otherwise be used for rebel movements.

This method seems preferable to regrouping wherever the density of communications, the presence of troops, and the nature of the terrain allow it.

2. The harkas generally proved to be very useful, especially because of their ability as scouts.

After first planning simply to reinforce each company or squadron by 20 or 30 harkas, it was decided to distinguish between: the harkas actually incorporated in units; and those who, living in their douars, work for the local administration. When the military force is decreased, these men should obviously remain where they are and come

° On the order of 1 douar to every 10–20 square kilometers [4–8 square miles].

under the responsibility of the SAS officers.[p] Admittedly this concept deviates from the official definition of the harkas: units organized for specific operations and for a limited time.[q]

3. Coordination of effort is undoubtedly an indispensable condition of success. One must adapt the various programs (building roads, improving housing and the water supply, extending the network of self-defending douars, etc.) to bring a common plan to fruition. The fact that the Sector Commander presently exercises civil powers facilitates this convergence of efforts, particularly in the way in which he can direct the spending of various funds. We should emphasize the great flexibility afforded by the Pilot funds, which, for the sake of advancing the over-all program, allowed a "revitalizing" of this or that service, which at a given moment was short of resources.

There still remains the task of perfecting—or rather of creating—a free [civilian] health service, whose duties are at present almost entirely handled by the Medical Corps. This is a particularly serious problem, since the reduction of military forces will by definition lead to a weakening of the resources available to the Medical Corps. At the moment, not a single civilian doctor is connected with the various SAS teams of the Pilot Area, and the least that can be said of the doctors of the Public Health Service is that they do not seem up to the task of relieving the military doctors, either because they are so few in number, or for other reasons.

4. An appendix contains some thoughts on the use of the loudspeaker and pamphlet company.

VI. *Conclusion*

In conclusion, we can do no more than repeat that the result of the operation is encouraging, but that its full value will reveal itself only in six months, after the military force has been further reduced.

We also regret that the operation could not be backed up, as had

[p] It appears reasonable to choose the *commune* as the administrative framework for these harkas. But it would then be necessary to increase the total strength of the SAS teams, so that the chief of the SAS could effectively command and control these "communal harkas."

[q] Directive No. 8 297/RM. 10/5 of May 20, 1957.

been hoped, by action in the adjoining sections of the Department of Orléansville.

It should further be pointed out that the self-defense policy showed its value in another part of the sector (north-northeast of Hillil and Bouguirat), where the local command, without the resources assigned to the Pilot Area, succeeded in creating in six months an area of pacification of almost 200 square kilometers [75 square miles], including approximately 30 armed douars: a result made possible only by the previous destruction of the rebel infrastructure—an operation pursued tenaciously and facilitated here, too, by a knowledge of the population based on identity papers.

Finally, though the effort seems to have been worthwhile, it was a considerable one, and the task left to the SAS teams when the other forces leave will be heavy indeed. It is essential to furnish the SAS with the means (personnel, matériel) for coping with these tasks.

Appendix: On the Use of the Loudspeaker and Pamphlet Company

Obviously the company was not employed in the Pilot Area according to the rules laid down in the manual: It was used in sections and not as a single unit.

This resulted first of all from the fact that the company arrived gradually (the first sections at the end of July, the rest at the beginning of November).

Since the operation had already begun throughout the entire Pilot Area, it was logical to pursue the psychological action everywhere, and not to make a special and temporary effort in this or that part of the Pilot Area. We wanted to establish and maintain contact rather than obtain a mass effect.

Furthermore, in an area of approximately 1,700 square kilometers [650 square miles], it seems preferable to assign the company by sections, placed at the disposal of the districts, rather than to operate for two or three weeks in a group of douars and then move on to neighboring douars, while abandoning the first group.

The use of the massed company should be reserved for the handling of important urban localities, like the Moslem suburbs of Mostaganem.

The success of Opération Pilote is difficult to evaluate. It has been described as one of the most remarkable strokes of counter-revolutionary warfare, a model of what might have been accomplished throughout Algeria if only the Army had received whole-hearted support.[2] Colonel Cazelles expressed himself more cautiously. His study makes plain that pacification is a term of very relative meaning, including such features as continued rebel movement through the area and continued need for information from the local inhabitants. What the French command had hoped to gain from Opération Pilote, apart from its experimental value, was tactical progress, not the end of fighting. It was sufficient if large-scale rebel activity could be prevented around Mostaganem, and if the area was secured against raids from the outside, so that the slow work of social and administrative reorganization could proceed undisturbed.

For a time, this was achieved. During fall and winter of 1958, the area remained quiet. The effort required had, however, proved too expensive to permit the simultaneous launching of similar operations in the fourteen other departments. Colonel Cazelles specifically mentions the absence of supporting action in the neighboring department of Orléansville. When in February, 1959, Opération Couronnes was launched to sweep the Ouarsenis Massif, south of the Pilot Area, numerous fellagahs were driven back into the Dahra Mountains, where a clandestine infrastructure was gradually reconstituting itself. That same spring, General Gambiez started his drive to pacify Oran Province—the western part of Algeria, stretching from the Moroccan border to Orléansville. In May, there was intense fighting along the Chéliff River, followed by engagements throughout the region, including the Department of Mostaganem. General Gambiez could nevertheless declare that Oranie had been pacified; a pronouncement somewhat amended by his superior, General Crepin, who stated that he considered Oranie "a zone of average FLN implantation." Clearly, however, the FLN had suffered hard blows, and during the first months of 1960, the northern half of Oran Province was among the safest regions in all Algeria.

Its peace was hardly lasting. So long as the population was willing to endure—and thus to support—the war, neither side could defeat the other, and the zigzag of fighting continued. The situation was perfectly summed up by General Le Pulloch, when he addressed generals and staff officers during his inspection tour in July, 1960:

> I want to caution generals and commanders of sectors against exaggerated optimism, which leads them to pretend that pacification has been achieved. This holds true for the Algérois and Oranie, where everything is felt to be in order, though twelve prominent men have just been butchered there, and terrorism is multiplying. Consequently, I suggest that you don't claim too much for yourselves by announcing that peace has returned to your areas. In most cases, this is only very superficially true.[3]

The incident General Le Pulloch referred to concerned the kidnaping and killing of twelve pro-French Moslems, together with a woman and two children, by a band of fellagahs southeast of Oran. Seven of the Moslems were municipal councilors who had just completed an orientation course. A few days later, the commander of an SAU section was shot in Mostaganem.[4] Another rebel commando had launched several attacks in the vicinity of Mostaganem during June, to which the French Army responded with sizable forces, supported by planes.[5]

Hard experience was convincing the Army of the strength of Commandant Hogard's proposition that insurrection can never be completely extinguished. Even in areas where the French authorities had undoubtedly regained a great deal of control, such as Saïda, in southern Oranie, and Bordj-bou-Arréridj, midway between Algiers and Constantine, a remnant of opposition could not be removed. What makes these two cases particularly thought-pro-voking is the fact that they had been subjected to very different kinds of treatment. The operation in Saïda was commanded by Colonel Marcel Bigeard, a paratrooper who with his toughness and romanticism personifies the modern French *mystique* of the soldier. "One must suffer to have the right to die," he wrote, char-acteristically, in an account of the Algerian War.[6] Bigeard pacified his zone in the *style para*—by predominantly military and police action. In Bordj-bou-Arréridj, on the contrary, Colonel Buis re-lied to a great extent on political and psychological measures. He urged expansion of the school system, supported medical and eco-nomic assistance, increased the authority of native leaders, and took care to establish and maintain friendly relations between his men and the population. In short, he did all that lay in the power of a local commander to build up his area's resistance to sub-version. But neither Bigeard nor Buis could succeed beyond a cer-tain stage, when the process of pacification—whether purely repres-sive or more political and psychological in nature—seemed to come up against an impassable barrier. "At this point," Serge Brom-berger, a well-informed and sympathetic observer, wrote, "whether for external or internal reasons, the situation worsens, then im-proves again, without the Army ever being able to cross the thresh-old for good."[7]

The existence of such a threshold in Algeria cannot be doubted. It was, however, dependent on the particular structure of which it formed a part, and if the structure were radically changed, the threshold might have disappeared. Let us review the task facing the 5th Cavalry Brigade at Mostaganem. Colonel Cazelles's units—totaling about 4,000 men—were to enter an area of 1,700 square kilometers [650 square miles] of difficult terrain, inhabited by 120,000 people, more than 97 per cent of them Moslems. They were to stamp out large-scale rebel activity, rebuild the social and economic life in the area, protect the civilian population, and by various means ranging from coercion to reforms win its adherence and support. In Mostaganem, the French enjoyed only partial and temporary success. But this is not to say that under different circumstances they could not have done better.

Relatively few units were committed at Mostaganem. With an addition of no more than one or two battalions of conscripts, the *quadrillage* system could have been strengthened and extended, while still leaving sufficient regulars available for mobile operations. Within the tighter network of territorial control, the self-defense douars would have' gained in effectiveness. But reinforcements were of doutbul benefit if they meant denuding the neighboring areas. The fact is that even such a sizable force as the 800,000 who were serving in Algeria by 1959, could only contain—not roll back—an insurgent movement operating among 9 million Moslems.[8]

Insufficient numbers might have been made up for by a stronger political program. As it was, in the early stages of Opération Pilote, the 2nd Loudspeaker and Pamphlet Company could offer the Moslems nothing more positive than social and economic reforms within an existing political framework. After the coup of May, 1958, the propaganda teams undoubtedly promoted integration, a message that by this late date was neither acceptable nor convincing. Only radical political change would have proved useful, and this lay far outside the competence of a local commander.

A policy equally beyond the authority of the man on the spot was that of large-scale resettlement. Clearly, if the French had been willing to pay the social and economic costs of depopulating the Pilot Area, total pacification would have been achieved. The local fellagahs, deprived of their popular base, would quickly have lost political significance and been left only the choice of withering on the vine or moving elsewhere. The burden to the French of such a program would, however, have been enormous. Only total resettlement could accomplish the purpose. The expense of moving and maintaining 117,000 Moslems would have fallen entirely on the Army and administration, while without their workers and customers, the European settlers would soon have become destitute as well. The depopulation of a zone that neither possessed strategic importance nor was a center of FLN activity would, of course, have been an admission of the bankruptcy of French policy. Finally, depopulating dozens of districts similar to Mostaganem would have meant the economic death of the country and the extermination of its Moslem inhabitants.

Barring a considerable strengthening of the military effort, a change in the political future offered Algeria, or the resettlement of the population, Opération Pilote was bound to achieve ephemeral success at best. This should not obscure its very considerable qualities. For one, the French command recognized that knowing the history of the local population, and understanding its present attitudes and ways, were not matters of academic interest but formed the prerequisite of effective propaganda and indeed of the whole program of pacification. The operation itself was carried out in remarkably undoctrinaire manner: The loudspeaker and pamphlet company, the harkas, the secret cadres were repeatedly employed contrary to official procedure. The whole was marked by unusual administrative and tactical flexibility, by the willingness—and ability—to cut across bureaucratic lines. To some extent, this is explained by the experimental nature of the action at Mostaganem; but much the same attitude can be observed in dozens of other Algerian zones, particularly during the later years of the war. The freedom of the French commands, their readiness to experiment, and the close integration of efforts is characteristic of most revolutionary movements in their combative period.

Chapter **7**

Sources and Implications

From the beginning, the proponents of *guerre révolutionnaire* claimed that their doctrine was not limited to the French situation alone, but possessed universal applicability. Far from simply reflecting the struggle between a waning colonial power and its dependencies, argued the theorists, *guerre révolutionnaire* outlined the most likely form war between East and West would take in the future—indeed, was already taking. Moreover, the methods of revolutionary or subversive war had been fully mastered by the East, while the West continued to be ill prepared to meet or to use them. Just as nuclear strategy cannot prevent classic or limited war, wrote General Chassin, so it cannot protect us from subversive war. "Without the slightest doubt, the most dangerous form of war for France, and perhaps for the West, is subversive war, because it can be waged with the least risk by an opponent acting through intermediaries, who can gradually deprive us of every strategic position in the world."[1] The French Army had fought this war unassisted for years; its experience in Indochina and Algeria constituted an important contribution to Western defense, if, said the French, the other members of the alliance could only be sufficiently alerted to the common danger to profit from them.

During the 1950's these claims met with little acceptance. Above all, France's partners desired an end to the Algerian conflict, and the reconstitution on the European continent of the mechanized divisions that had been withdrawn and retrained for action against the fellagahs. French operations were studied with a view to learning particular lessons—the usefulness of helicopters against guerrillas, for example—rather than to understanding the underlying concept. Some interest in the doctrine of *guerre révolutionnaire* was fostered by the attendance of NATO officers at French staff courses, visits to the Algerian battle areas, and the publication of articles by Hogard, Souyris, and others in American and European military journals.[2] Recently, this interest has considerably expanded in the United States, in the wake of the country's new concern with armed subversion in Central America and Southeast Asia. Even now, however, attention concentrates on techniques, while the problem of their implications in the realms of politics and grand strategy tends to be overlooked or glossed over. But to ignore the political techniques of a politico-military doctrine, or to argue that the French Army's methods in the field were appropriate, but were vitiated by the political situation in France, is as misleading as to deduce the doctrine's over-all value solely from the effectiveness of certain of its techniques.

An evaluation of the usefulness to the West of the doctrine of *guerre révolutionnaire* must be based on more than a study of its tactics. To discover whether the doctrine—despite its failure against the Algerians—is actually international in scope, we should address ourselves to three additional problems. To begin with, we should inquire more deeply into its antecedents. Its proponents argue that the theory was evolved to meet a specific threat against the West. But is it inconceivable that something very like this doctrine might have been developed even if the Indochinese and Algerian wars had never occurred? To put it differently, to what extent was the doctrine patterned by a reaction to the forces of a new nationalism, to anticolonialism, and Communism, and to what extent by inherent tendencies in the French past and present? Secondly, we should consider the political viability of the doctrine. Does it lend itself to forming part of a balanced national policy, or is it inherently dangerous to the stability of government and nation? Finally, we should ask whether the over-all strategic analysis by the theorists of *guerre révolutionnaire* is accurate.

The French loss of Indochina was the immediate cause that gave rise to the development of the doctrine of *guerre révolutionnaire* as a decisive factor in national policy. The Army's defeat by the Vietnamese has sometimes been called a trauma : an experience of such violence and significance that it radically affects everything that follows. To describe the reactions of large social organisms in the language of individual psychology is usually pointless, but here the term seems not wholly inappropriate. The defeat did rouse the Army, or, more correctly, groups within it, to the recognition that against a politically sophisticated enemy fighting on his native ground, conventional methods of colonial repression were insufficient. More important, it served as an insistent call to action. What the defeat did not indicate was exactly how future conflicts should be fought. That is, the doctrine of *guerre révolutionnaire* was not an inevitable outcome of the Indochinese experience— something French military commentators have tended to overlook.

Other armies at the time were facing revolutionary movements without developing a comparable doctrine. During the early years of the war in Indochina, Chiang was still fighting the Chinese Communists, the Greek Government was fighting General Markos, Malaya and the Philippines were contending with serious insurrections; but none of the incumbents, whether they eventually won or lost, evolved a response as intense and encompassing as the French. In these and other internal wars, somewhat similar experiences led to very dissimilar results.

A decisive spur to the growth of the French doctrine was a willingness to learn from the enemy that went far beyond the usual adjustment to new or special situations. Officers began to engage in an energetic, almost passionate inquiry into enemy doctrine, particularly into the writings of Mao Tse-tung. But since they were interested less in objective analysis than in gaining the quickest possible operation payoff, their studies tended to be superficial. Contrary to their view, Mao's writings do not, after all, add up to a general theory of modern war—nor had that been his intention. Generally, his papers and speeches were prompted by particular political or military problems encountered by the Communists, and were designed to define policy, convince dissidents, instruct subordinates. His interpretations of European and African wars were contradictory and ill informed—which mattered little, since their function was simply to lend weight to his arguments with his fellow Chinese. That Mao's policy statements and exhortations were occasioned by specific events need not, of course, limit their wider applicability; but some appreciation at least of their context is required to understand them, and this Mao's French admirers largely ignored. They studied him as though he were not the leader of a revolution but a Lloyd or a Jomini, a maker of systems, and for illustrations of his theories they drew on his campaigns, which not surprisingly bore out his texts to perfection. Possibly they felt that by the very virtue of Mao's Marxism, his thought must be universal; certainly they imagined his hand raised against them everywhere—in Algeria no less than in Asia. They lost sight of the fact that despite the similarities that could be traced between the condition of the Japanese in China and that of the French in Indochina, Mao and Giap fought very different wars, and that the success of the Vietnamese owed far less to Mao's formulations of military theory than to China's political and material support. It was easier to emphasize the potency of "ideology" and of new techniques than to recognize the enemy's physical and strategic superiority, and thus admit that France, however strong her determination to gain victory, was too weak to have won this war. Moreover, there were certain elements in their military tradition that made the French recognize features in the enemy camp that appealed to them. These elements may be likened to inherited predilections, dormant but not extinct, that become active again in periods of great stress. Dien Bien Phu and the Geneva Conference provided such a crisis.

What were the decisive reactions to the defeat in Indochina? On the one hand, disappointment with the government and the nation for failing to give the Army the massive support it deemed necessary. On the other, the determination to put into practice certain ideas acquired during the fighting. First, the significance of ideology, both as a guide to action, directing the grand lines of the conflict, and as a weapon, an item in each soldier's equipment. Not a few officers in Vietnamese prison camps had observed the use of this weapon at close range—in the form of re-education. Equally taken to heart was the importance of economic and social reforms in the pursuit of the war, and the desirability of close integration of the political and military commands. How far this latter had been achieved by the enemy was largely hidden from French eyes; what was apparent were the defects on their own side—political, social, and moral—which became more glaring at each remove from the battle zones. Further, the French had become strongly attracted to Mao's concept of the political functions of the military—the Army's role as an instrument of propaganda and as a preparatory school for future administrators and officials. Finally, they became convinced that in wars of the post-colonial era civilians could no longer be ignored: By persuasion or coercion they had to be brought into the fight on one's side.

All these were ideas difficult for the conventional military mind
to accept and act upon. It was swayed more by certain less revolutionary and more immediately convincing operational experiences, which demonstrated the power against a modern, motorized
army of small units, operating cross-country, receiving their intelligence and much of their supply from the population. Such an opponent could scarcely be defeated by pushing sizable, heavily
equipped forces deep into his territory, where their supply lines
were easily cut, their detached units ambushed, the main body itself gradually choked off. Needed instead was a network of blockhouses and posts, reinforced by mobile detachments, covering a
population whose allegiance had been won. Only offensive operations based on this kind of security stood any chance of lasting
success.

These political and military conclusions—Raymond Aron summarized them as "the responsibility of the regime, the historic role
of subversive war"—were invested with an outsized measure of
emotional force because, as has already been suggested, they recalled a number of factors in the French Army's past.[3]

The military concepts, for one, reverted to techniques developed
and codified by French colonial officers before World War I. In
the course of French expansion overseas, the conventional method
of thrusting infantry columns deep into native territory had
proved of limited value. The columns occupied administration
and communication centers with little difficulty, but they left the
countryside relatively untouched and therefore were unable to
prevent banditry and political unrest. As long as the Third Republic was more concerned with laying claim to territory than
with committing itself to the expense and risks of full-scale administration, this was not too serious; but as colonial policy became
one of actual rather than nominal control, different methods were
required. A new generation of colonial officers—the generation of
the future Marshals Gallieni and Lyautey—agreed that for puni-

tive purposes the column still had its uses, though Bugeaud, the conqueror of Algeria, had already said that in Africa an expedition without occupation left no trace; thorough "pacification," however, could be achieved only by meshing unconventional military techniques with attempts to win the natives' confidence while reorganizing important features of their political, social, and economic existence. By the 1890's, these ideas had met with considerable success in Asia and Africa, and the new doctrine became accepted.[4]

Its outstanding military characteristic was the gradual advance on a wide front instead of a single deep penetration. Columns were still employed to break up large enemy concentrations and for other special missions, but the emphasis lay on the *tache d'huile,* or oil-stain technique—a methodical, necessarily slow expansion of French control. First a chain, then a network, of posts was established, each unit of which served as a nucleus of military, administrative, and propaganda action—the last being highly important, since, in Lyautey's phrase, the posts were to be "centers of attraction rather than repulsion."[5] Patrols between them prevented the re-establishment of opposition in the intermediary areas. As control was extended, villages in·the relatively secure zones were armed and made responsible for their own defense; concurrently, natives were organized into auxiliary Army units, so that a large part of the population became committed to the French cause.

The military phase of occupation, or pacification, was prepared and accompanied by political action. Natives in as yet unconquered regions were subjected to propaganda stressing the twin themes that life was better under French rule and that only France was strong enough to keep the peace. Whenever suitable, segments of the population were turned against their rulers, or tribal leaders were set against one another. As the Army established control, it imposed its administration, which extended from the purely military realm of defense to the maintenance of roads, the building of

schools and medical centers, the collecting of taxes, and the handing down of justice. These activities formed an integral part of
the military advance. As Lyautey wrote:

> When the occupation of a new territory is decided on for political or
> administrative reasons, we never proceed by "spear thrusts of col-
> umns," keeping the problems of organization in abeyance until the
> end of the operation; on the contrary, all the elements of final occupa-
> tion and organization are ensured in advance. . . . It is indeed an
> "organization that marches."[6]

For the smooth progress of pacification, close cooperation between civil and military authority was obviously essential. The
best way to ensure this, argued the colonial officers, was to create
actual unity of command, placing military and administrative responsibility in the same hands, not only at the summit of the official hierarchy but on lower levels, as well. "The fundamental doctrine of the sector," Lyautey declared, "rests on the identity of
territorial command and military command in regions that must
be maintained under military rule"—this identity reaching down to
company level.[7] It hardly needs saying that the individuals holding this power were to be soldiers, not civilians. They were, however, to be officers of a special type. The "pure" soldier was rejected as being useful only in Europe, where a meaningful division
between military and nonmilitary duties could be drawn, and
where the former could be satisfactorily fulfilled by sticking to the
manual. Overseas, on the contrary, men were needed with an interest in political, social, and economic affairs, who could impro-
vise, and who in their military tasks were not specialists, but able
to command a company, run an intelligence service, organize a
supply system. While held to general directives, they were expected to manage the affairs of their sectors in their own way, pay-
ing greater attention to particular local conditions than to the
detailed orders emanating from the ministries in Paris.

The threat such ideas represented to subordination and civilian control was obvious, but despite resistance in the Army and in Parliament, the *officier-administrateur* became accepted, and it was he who conquered and ruled large tracts of France's second colonial empire. His doctrine survived well into the twentieth century. When a few months before the outbreak of war in 1939, a French general discussed recent Army operations in Morocco, he was still able to do so in the language of Gallieni and Lyautey; their theses of the military significance of nonmilitary measures remained the basis of the French effort.[8] World War II pushed the colonial experience into the background; it was gradually reverted to as conventional methods proved ineffective against the Vietnamese. Many of the significant components of *guerre révolutionnaire*— unity of command (which, in effect, meant military domination over civilian affairs), the importance of propaganda and of social and economic measures, the system of close territorial control— could be found in various stages of development in the theory and practice of the Colonial Army before 1914.

The tradition of the Colonial Army, however, had more to offer the vanquished of Dien Bien Phu than operational doctrine. Its leading figures possessed a very pronounced sense of mission, which they passed on to their collaborators, disciples, and successors. To a great extent, their attitude was a French expression of that peculiar mixture of romanticism and hardheaded self-interest —equally prevalent in the England of Cecil Rhodes and the United States of Theodore Roosevelt—that made up nineteenth-century imperialism. With their patriotic desire for the expansion of French power and prestige in the world went a certain sense of responsibility for the native populations who became involved in the process. Here, too, the French were only following a general trend of the age; where they struck out on their own, however, was in not reserving their paternalism to Africa and Asia, but in wishing to extend it to metropolitan France, as well. To be sure, the dream of regenerating the homeland through overseas endeavor was not always absent among Anglo-Saxon imperialists, but an influential group of French officers carried the thought further, and the considerably less stable political environment in which they lived was conducive to the serious development of such ideas.

The replacement of the Second Empire by the Third Republic, the conflict with Rome, the increasing industrialization of the country, all were pushing French society in directions distasteful to officers, who despite their loyalty to the Republic could not deny their Catholic and traditionalist backgrounds. At the same time, these radical developments offered new means for shaping the attitudes of the population. In particular, the change of emphasis from a professional army to universal military conscription meant that hundreds of thousands of young men would for a time come under the close supervision of officers, who were thus provided with a heaven-sent opportunity to fortify them against the anarchic tendencies of the day. For this task, the aloof officer of old, who knew his horses better than the men in his platoon, was entirely unsuited. A new type of leader was wanted, who concerned himself with the welfare and the state of mind of his subordinates, and by personal example, interviews, and lectures, impressed on their minds the desired personal and civic values. The most important expression of this concept is again Lyautey's.

In 1891, shortly before leaving for a tour of duty in Madagascar, Lyautey published an article on the social duties of the French officer, which became as famous as its later counterpart on the Army's colonial tasks.[9] In it, the young commandant pointed to the need for indoctrinating the conscripts, criticized the narrow professionalism, the snobbery and "anglomania" too prevalent in the officer corps, and called on his comrades to acknowledge their dual role of leaders in war, educators in peacetime. The content of the indoctrination he did not spell out, but its main features emerge clearly between the lines: patriotism, nationalism, *revanche* for the defeat of 1870, social peace, a disciplined selfless people. In themselves, these ideas were of an unexceptionable if highly conservative cast; the plea for the Army's involvement in education, however, touched on decidedly dangerous ground, and its appearance in print caused considerable discussion and criticism. The immediate influence of Lyautey's theses was on individuals rather than on the Ministry of War, their effect on the relationship between officer and man remained slight; but his arguments, and those of his supporters in the Army, the universities, and the Church became part of the intellectual equipment of numerous "thinking" soldiers. To the later observer, it is obvious that *l'officier-administrateur* and *l'officier-educateur* were related ideals: the one renouncing an easy career in Europe to struggle in the colonies for the sake of French power and the highest values of French civilization; the other striving among an undisciplined and corrupt society to purify France, to render the mass of Frenchmen worthy of their country and of the sacrifices made for their sake. They form two aspects of the same longing for a regenerating elite, which tests and proves itself in military service before leading the nation to new grandeur.

In more virulent form, the thesis of a regeneration of France emanating from the Army reappeared in military circles in the 1930's. It contributed to the meager ideological store of the Vichy regime. Given a new lease on life by the right's panic fear of Bolshevism, it survived the coming of the Fourth Republic, until gradually faith in the messianic power of the Army and willingness to use the Army for a *coup d'état* merged in the activist groups of the 1950's. These, as was pointed out earlier, were by no means recruited solely from the Catholic right; but the emergence of such a near-seditious movement as the Cité Catholique showed that the long-established link between Catholic conservatives and anti-Republicanism persisted in the services. From 1956 on, the Cité organized a network of clandestine cells "for study and action" to spread its militant anti-Communist, anti-Republican message among the armed forces. The number of members and their identity were kept secret; they appear to have been particularly well represented in the traditionally legitimist branches of the service, the Cavalry and the Navy. In 1959, two editors of *Le Monde* suggest, more than 100 cells existed in Algeria, each with a membership of between 5 and 8 (both officers and other ranks), while there were 4,000 subscribers to the monthly journal of the movement *Verbe*.[10] Annual meetings of the organization were attended by such personalities as Marshal Juin, Generals Weygand and Chassin—the latter one of the first Western students of Mao, and a strong believer in the power of psychological warfare—and the neofascist Dr. Lefèvre, who was to become implicated in the trial of the generals. The preaching of the Cité Catholique was anti-Republican and counterrevolutionary in the most classic sense. It proclaimed that the Revolution of 1789 was the root of all present evil. From this it followed that it was necessary "to fight against everything that sprang from the Revolution, against its 'sons' who are the liberals, the radicals, the socialists and Communists, and naturally the FLN . . . loyalty to the nation has its roots in religious faith, and nowhere else."[11]

Although their religious convictions made it difficult for right-wing Catholics to subscribe to an extreme program of psychological warfare and re-education, they generally found it possible to cooperate closely with its advocates. Some had a foot in each camp—General Chassin, for one. Another was the most prominent French propagandist of psychological warfare, Georges Sauge. In his recent study on the Catholic Church in France, William Bosworth suggests that at present Sauge is still one of the key men among Catholics of the extreme right, and continues:

> Sauge, a former Communist Party member, has organized a "Center for the Advanced Study of Social Psychology," and a movement called *Force Psychologique*. This movement seems to have a certain influence in the French Army. . . . The main activity of Sauge is agitation against

Communism, "Marxism," and left-wing Catholicism. . . . Recently his importance has been enhanced by giving regular courses in psychological warfare to reserve army officers. . . . Sauge has received support from such political figures as Georges Bidault, General Chassin, Poujade, and the corporatist Dr. Lefèvre, as well as from some of the more rock-ribbed conservatives among the hierarchy.[12]

The psychological ideas that Sauge presented to the armed forces—in talks to military academies and groups of regulars, as well as to reservists—were adopted eagerly by the Army's *action psychologique* groups.[13] Fundamental to his argument was the supposition that people could be conditioned to do, and to believe in, practically anything, and that it was the right of the state to exploit this truth.

This is a long way from Lyautey's plea that officers instill patriotism and social obedience in the young citizens temporarily in their charge. Nor can the self-denying loyalty of the colonial soldier be confused with the adventurism of the Chassins and Sauges. But the generations are bridged by attitudes held in common by both: dissatisfaction with democratic society and parliamentary government, belief in an elite. The French collapse in 1940 before a disciplined Germany spurred these feelings. The defeat was blamed on a dissolute, decadent society by men who never thought of looking into themselves and weighing the justice of Marc Bloch's comment that one reason for the disaster was the officers' loss of faith in the people and the nation. In 1940, as after 1870, the idea of *revanche* captured the right; this time, however, the target for revenge was not the external enemy but the internal opposition. By coupling the symbols of a universal faith with a social program calling for "an authoritarian traditionalist Christian order which explicitly repudiates the postulates of liberal individualism," right-wing Catholicism to some extent filled the ideological needs of the doctrine of *guerre révolutionnaire*.[14] By its alliance with activist groups, it helped push the doctrine into open opposition to the state.

Once more the Army's past helped shape its reaction to the Indochinese trauma. The doctrine of *guerre révolutionnaire* demanded ideological cohesion and unity of purpose between armed forces, government, and people. The Army could try to bring about solidarity by persuasion. If it failed, the proponents of the doctrine came to argue, the Army had the right to impose its ideals, since, as an article in *Verbe* put it, "the Army's concept of the common good was superior to that of the state." This was not an unlikely conclusion to reach for officers, who once before in their careers had been forced to decide between conflicting loyalties. After the fall of France, each was faced with the choice of giving his adherence to the De Gaulle government or to Vichy. For those who pinned their hopes on Pétain as guarantor of French sovereignty, a further period of trial reached its climax with the Allied landings in North Africa and the Nazi occupation of the free zone of France in November, 1942. Whatever the officer's decision, it repudiated claims of authority that were acknowledged by thousands of his comrades; and these personal decisions could not but help diminish faith in the principle of unquestioned obedience. After 1945, during a period of social change at home and renewed fighting overseas, the traditional service standards of discipline and subordination could not be fully restored. As in the years of defeat, men stood in judgment over their government and their military superiors, deciding when to obey and when to sabotage authority. By 1957, the then Army Chief of Staff, General André Zeller, could write in the *Revue de Défense Nationale,* the country's most prestigious military journal: "In the global crisis in which we are now involved, and considering our likely enemies, an Army can no longer obey or sacrifice itself for words such as 'duty' or 'discipline,' which purely by themselves are, to put it bluntly, meaningless to the Army."[15] The experience of the Vichy era, in many ways akin to civil war, henceforth made disobedience easier to contemplate, resort to, and condone.[16]

That some components of the doctrine of *guerre révolution-naire* are deeply rooted in the French past is neither surprising nor does it argue necessarily against the efficacy of the doctrine. It is, however, important to recognize the considerable extent of this debt to tradition, and to understand in detail what it consisted of. It is equally important to note that in some respects the tradition was not one of success.

Failure does not characterize the military techniques of the Gallienis and Lyauteys, which presage in principle—and often in actual execution—many of the operational concepts of the doctrine. Their political techniques, and the military solution of the problem of civil-military cooperation, are, however, more ambiguous: If pushed beyond a certain stage, they inevitably compete with the authority of the state. The third factor outlined, the Army's sense of mission, has in its long history led only to failure, contributing to, rather than alleviating, the internal conflicts of the nation. In its link with authoritarian and neofascist schools of thought, which constitute the most immediate inspiration of the doctrine's ideology, it brought France to the edge of civil war.

Is it accidental that so many of the theorists and supporters of the doctrine of *guerre révolutionnaire* are found among the leaders of the various putsches and rebellions that shook France during the past years? The list of implicated officers is impressive. To name only the most prominent: General Zeller was sentenced to fifteen years' imprisonment for being one of the chiefs of the April, 1961, revolt. His fellow conspirator, General Challe, who lectured his judges on the wisdom of Mao Tse-tung, received the same sentence. The close tie between General Chassin, one of the originators of the doctrine, and right-wing extremists has already been noted. His involvement went far beyond arranging lectures and writing activist propaganda. In the spring of 1958, he organized a plot against the government, and after the 13th of May he attempted to raise guerrillas in the Lyons area.[17] Another pioneer, Colonel Lacheroy, once described as the Gustave Le Bon of psychological warfare, was condemned to death *in absentia* for the part he played in the 1961 revolt, as were Colonels Argoud (later captured), Broizat, Gardes, and Godard—each of whom had made contributions to the theory and practice of *guerre révolutionnaire.* Godard, chief of intelligence and security in Algiers from 1958 until February, 1960, became one of the heads of the OAS, together with Colonel Argoud, the author of what appears to have been the most comprehensive plan of police- and thought-control of the Algerian population. His OAS pamphlet, *Le problème algérien—solution française,* is referred to in the following pages. Gardes, tried but acquitted for his part in the "Week of the Barricades," had during the 1950's attempted to synthesize Communist techniques and Christianity, and organized study groups on the Christian use of terror. Broizat, once a Catholic, then a Communist, finally a violently anti-Communist theorist of psychological warfare, has been described as "an apostle of total war, which he defines, justifies, and practices."[18] In the hands of these and similar men, the body of politico-military methods they had originally developed to defeat the external enemies of France became the intellectual inspiration and justification of internal war.[19]

That in very many cases the same officers who had elaborated the system of *guerre révolutionnaire* later took up arms against the state constitutes a heavy indictment of the doctrine. The extremists are not wholly representative, however. The diversity of interests and motives behind the doctrine, as well as its failure to evolve a powerful ideology, assured the existence of widely differing attitudes. The moderation of Colonel Bonnet's writings has already been mentioned. Somewhat akin to his position was that of the prominent civilian contributor to the *Revue de Défense Nationale* Claude Delmas, whose little book *La guerre révolutionnaire* played an important role in spreading the new ideas among the public. But while stressing the gravity of subversive war, Bonnet and Delmas showed caution when it came to recommending counterstrategies, and both were concerned with the dangers to the user inherent in extreme techniques. Their views undoubtedly were—and are—shared by many individuals in the services and in civilian life.

A spokesman of a very different group—the professional soldiers who had succumbed to a demonology of Communism and nationalism—was Colonel Roger Trinquier, an officer who contributed much to the pacification of the Algiers Casbah. His book *La guerre moderne* (1961) combines imaginative tactical analysis with a view of the world that is as primitive as it is factually wrong.[20] Far from laying claim to the universality implied in the work's title, the writer makes the important point that *guerre révolutionnaire* is a doctrine specifically suited to colonial and developing territories. His discussion of counterguerrilla techniques is based on wide experience, and deserves attention. When he leaves the realm of tactics, however, his objectivity and good sense vanish. To Colonel Trinquier, revolutionary war is total war, admitting neither compromise nor negotiation, since the cause he represents has justice on its side while the enemy's position is totally wrong. According to this concept, the Algerians fought France not for their own self-interest, enlightened or otherwise, but because they were deceived and terrorized. On the other hand, the French reason for carrying on the war was "to give the Algerians their freedom."[21] If the rightness of French motives was absolute, so was the justice of their techniques. "The firmness of repression was reserved only for our enemies. The population never doubted this. . . ."[22] In its potential for irresponsible violence, this naïveté was only a short step removed from the cynical nihilism that came to dominate the doctrine by the early 1960's.

As far back as the middle years of the preceding decade, tracts had circulated among French units in North Africa, metropolitan France, and Germany that sought to apply the theories of *guerre révolutionnaire* to the conquest of power within France. The reasoning in these clandestine texts was simple enough. Our enemies' greatest weapon, the argument ran, is their ideological solidarity, which renders possible both their effective political maneuvers and their successes on the battlefield—guerrillas not being able to maintain themselves among a hostile population. To defeat them, we must match their ideological strength; but this we cannot do under the present liberal, republican system, under which our will to fight is weakened by corruption, decadence, and treason. To win, we must first reconstruct our own ideological and physical base— metropolitan France. Revolutionary war abroad must be met by counterrevolutionary war; subversion and incipient Communist revolution at home by counterrevolution.

The most interesting and influential among these tracts appeared anonymously in 1957 under the title *Contre-révolution, stratégie et tactique*.[23] A pamphlet of about 145 pages, it was distributed to thousands of officers, who could find in its pages both philosophic arguments that justified insurrection against the Fourth Republic, and an analysis of the methods to be employed. The ideology voiced was that of the extreme activist and Catholic right. The pamphlet sought to foster what it termed the unchanging, nonevolutionary human spirit, to re-establish "the equilibrium between the three basic social institutions—family, state, property," and to protect against subversion the eternal French values and the mission granted France by Providence.[24] The enemy threatening these ideals it identified as international Communism; the operational targets for its counterattack were the legal authorities and the so-called "revolutionary forces" in France.

The pamphlet agrees with the doctrine of *guerre révolutionnaire* in considering revolutionary war an expression of the global Communist conspiracy. The only effective way to counter it is by politico-military action, which first secures its home base: "The Army fights in vain if the political conditions needed for its operations are not fulfilled."[25] These conditions are:

"1. Civilian participation is indispensable to the success of a counterrevolutionary insurrection.

"2. The Army must transform itself. From a purely military organization it must change into a politico-military force that participates in the counterrevolution.

"3. A unified command over civil and military authorities must be created. . . . This unity of command should be implanted at all echelons throughout the country, forming a single hierarchic pyramid of responsible chiefs.

"4. A political program must be drawn up, covering all problem areas of revolutionary war, in particular: psychological and ideological action, social reforms, military action. . . ."[26]

The counterrevolution can take the offensive only after lengthy political and psychological preparation of the people. It must represent the people's aspirations "whether these are voiced or not." In the past, the failure of insurrections has generally been due to a premature recourse to overt military action. To succeed, an insurrection should "cap a political and psychological campaign that has attempted to bring about:

"1. The friendly neutrality of the majority of the people.

"2. The psychological and material support of the police and the armed forces.

"3. The possibility of establishing an infrastructure of political and military controls necessary to support its further moves."[27]

Having analyzed the general concepts of counterrevolutionary war, the pamphlet proceeds to develop its strategic principles. Lenin, Trotsky, and Mao are the major intellectual sources, but their arguments are adapted to the needs of a small, industrialized country, in which space cannot be traded for time. The most suggestive section of the text—"Defense and Offense"—points out that

early defeats may actually prove to be an advantage to the counterrevolution: As long as the movement has not reached the stage of
open fighting, it controls forces that are only potential; these are
activated once fighting begins. The text continues:

> Echoing Mao, we claim that as soon as counterrevolutionary troops
> are engaged, they turn *ipso facto* into a force for propaganda and or-
> ganization of the counterrevolutionary movement. This conception
> creates a new way of looking at things, according to which we should
> prepare for and judge the loss of a position and all other partial
> checks, because they are nothing but temporary and limited set-
> backs . . . a defeat still constitutes a victory for the counterrevolu-
> tion. . . .

From a potential force, the counterrevolution turns into an active
force, with new means for gaining popular support and building
a revolutionary base.[28] Not unreasonably, it has been suggested
that the decision to activate the Secret Army Organization after
the collapse of the 1961 putsch was influenced by considerations of
this nature, which aimed not at immediate victory but at the creation of an atmosphere favorable to insurrection throughout Algeria and France.

The military or quasi-military techniques with which the counterrevolution fights are enumerated in the text as terror, guerrilla warfare, and general insurrection—which last incorporates
both regular and irregular military action. On the second and
third subjects, the pamphlet simply repeats the reasoning of the
contributors to the *Revue Militaire d'Information* and the *Revue
de Défense Nationale;* the discussion on terror is of necessity somewhat more original. It is assumed that the basic function of psychological and physical terror is to destroy people's "atavistic
faith" in the government, and to prepare them to support the
struggle for a new order.[29] The Communists find terror completely
acceptable, but it cannot be employed by the counterrevolution
since "in contrast to revolution and subversion, counterrevolution

seeks to install a natural authority. The [counterrevolutionary] movement does not try to take hold of the population, but rather to liberate it, and engage it in the fight against a foreign power for the common national good. At no time can the people be the enemy."[30]

The categorical rejection of terror is however immediately qualified: "If it does become necessary to make an example, it should be done in the spirit of order and justice." Terror is permitted when it is a matter of protecting the people against exactions or sanctions of the legal or revolutionary authorities, or of backing up the counterrevolutionary forces during the early stages of the takeover of power.[31] The equivocations of the text do not hide the fact that the anonymous authors accept the use of discriminate terror, the assassination of more or less carefully selected individuals—loyal officials and soldiers, political opponents, presumably even hostages.

The last part of the tract consists of two exhaustive analyses of the prospects for counterrevolution—in the world and in France, the inhabitants of each being divided into two opposing camps. Among the presumed "troops, reserves, and allies" of the revolution in France are ranged all political parties of the Fourth Republic, groups in the civil service and in the university faculties, labor unions, people favoring the separation of Church and state, not to mention Communists and Communist sympathizers. The counterrevolutionary cause is supposedly backed by businessmen, shopkeepers, peasants, devout Christians, the greater part of the clergy, the Army, the French in Algeria, and patriotic organizations.[32] The text concludes by advising the reader that the work he has just studied is "a weapon, designed as such, and to be used as such. It would be insane to break a sword and fight only with the hilt or only with the blade; the counterrevolutionary weapon, too, forms a whole, to be used whole and without restrictions."[33] Once again we encounter the argument that nothing less than a total effort will be sufficient. Here legal and subversive proponents of *guerre révolutionnaire* are in complete agreement: Participants in revolutionary war cannot pick and choose their methods; they must all be used. Psychological warfare without indoctrination of one's own supporters is as ineffective as a political maneuver not backed by terror. For any one method to achieve lasting success, the entire armory of techniques must be exploited.

The arguments developed during the late 1950's in *Contre-révolution, stratégie et tactique,* and by similar extremist publications and groups, were given a new dynamic by the emergence of the OAS as an independent fighting force after the failure of the 1961 putsch. Anti-Communism was claimed by its leaders to be the basic motive of the organization. "The war in Algeria," Colonel Argoud wrote, "forms an episode in the struggle between the Communist and Western worlds. Unexpectedly breaking out in an era of major strategic importance, at a crucial period of decolonization and economic competition, its outcome is a matter of life and death not only for France but for the entire West." The reasons for the French setbacks in Indochina and Algeria Argoud located in "ideological confusion," "intellectual masochism," "an excess of civilization." To recover the initiative, "France must reform its own worst faults, whether these lie in the realm of morality, or in the areas of civil or military organization."[34]

It is difficult to identify the concrete political program behind these generalizations. Throughout 1961 and the early months of 1962, the OAS fought under the slogan *"Algérie française,"* many of its members rejecting even the idea of integration for that of colonial possession pure and simple. The reconstitution of French government and society was envisaged along corporate lines, with political parties and labor unions suppressed, and an extensive militia system binding together a state similar in character to fascist Italy or Vichy France, though apparently some leaders were reluctant to go to this length. The military policy of the OAS was more clear-cut. To quote Argoud once more, "The French Army has spent fifteen years working toward an effective and consistent doctrine of revolutionary war. This has been evolved, but some of the senior officers are still far from accepting the new ideas." For Argoud and his companions, it was now a question of putting the doctrine of *guerre révolutionnaire* into practice not only against the FLN but against the legal authorities as well. After the OAS failed to win over a significant portion of the French forces in Algeria, it attempted to establish maquis in the countryside. When this, too, failed, its formations reverted to selective terror, mainly in the cities and towns, and then finally to indiscriminate terror, slaying Moslem supporters and opponents of the FLN alike. In this downward process, it followed the development that the doctrine outlined for a declining insurgent force: inability to regularize operations, return to guerrilla warfare, and then to terror. The Indochinese and Algerians, however, had never for long made the mistake of pinning their prospects on unselective destruction. Besides, they had employed terror to achieve an end commensurate with this technique: to render the authorities' position untenable, to force them out of the country, while the OAS used terror to compel the French to stay. In its hands, the doctrine of *guerre révolutionnaire* finally resulted in complete anarchy, destruction without political purpose, expressing nothing but frustration.

Whether this was an inevitable outcome of the doctrine is a moot point. Certainly it lay close to hand. Too many individuals who developed its theories were political adventurers. More important, the central concepts of pacification and of subversion are either identical or at a short remove from one another. At the very least, it is difficult to avoid the conclusion that the doctrine of *guerre révolutionnaire* contains a high potential of political explosiveness, a characteristic that should severely limit its usefulness as a counterstrategy for other countries.

The matter may not be that simple, however. It has been repeatedly argued that the weaknesses of the Fourth Republic left the Army no choice but to act on its own. This point of view is by no means limited to officers or to the extreme right. It has been put forward by such men as Raoul Girardet and Jean-Marie Domenach, a member of the Catholic left and editor of *Esprit*. In an important article in *Foreign Affairs,* M. Domenach wrote that the French military leadership "demanded that the State define a policy and hold to it. As the State was weak and divided, the Army naturally substituted itself for the State. . . ."[35] If this were the case, it might be thought that despite its anti-Republican origins and connections, the doctrine of *guerre révolutionnaire* does not express a revolutionary point of view, and that it has little bearing on the military's involvements in politics, which were rather forced on the Army from the outside.

But what do the abstractions "Army" and "weak and divided State" stand for in this context? By no means all armed forces of the Republic became politicized during the 1950's, let alone participated in putsches. Yet unless the majority of officers and men, which rejected all attempts to shape policy, is considered unpatriotic or blind, it is difficult to speak of the Army being compelled to substitute itself for the state. Besides, was it really the weakness of the regime that some officers found so objectionable? Events since 1958 indicate the opposite. As the Fifth Republic gradually acquired authority, as the government in metropolitan France gathered strength, opposition from these groups did not cease. On the contrary. The putsch of 1961 was not a protest against the feebleness of General de Gaulle's policies, but an attempt to change them. When sections of the armed forces disagree with a government's plans and try to impose their own, their actions scarcely come under the category of filling a vacuum.

In much the same vein, it has been argued for years that the French Army could not withdraw from Algeria because hundreds of officers had personally given the Moslems their word of honor that they would never be abandoned. As M. Domenach put it in 1961, "The Army will not stand by passively and see its military successes wiped out by a political victory of the FLN, nor will it ever resign itself to abandoning to enemy reprisals the 160,000 harkas . . . whom it has enrolled and the Moslem civilians who have collaborated with it. The Army would consider this much more than a political impossibility—it would be a crime, a betrayal of a word of honor."[36] This prediction was based on questionable premises, and it turned out to be wrong. Whether the officers' assurances had been exacted by, or thrust upon, their recipients must remain in doubt. What is certain is that no modern government can conduct national policy according to the tenets of personal honor professed by a faction of its servants. These particular tenets, moreover, are suspect. The oaths given to the Moslems during the 1950's did nothing to protect them against the indiscriminate French terror of 1961 and 1962. Presumably, the officers who swore the oath and the OAS killers were not the same men; but the policy of indiscriminate terror—terror, that is, in which the victims were chosen not for their political preferences, but solely on the ground of being non-European—was directed by French officers, and not renounced by their titular chief, General Salan. Nor did the former heads of the 5es Bureaux, now gone into hiding, find it objectionable that the Moslem schools, which the SAS had built with so much energy and devotion, became in the spring of 1962 the favorite targets of the OAS. The claims that governmental weakness required the Army to seize power, that its honor compelled it to stay in Algeria, formed part of a maze of deception and self-deception that hid the intention of civilian and military groups to change policy by extraconstitutional means.

Chapter **8**

Conclusion

Failure is a poor recommendation. But failure may be due to outside circumstances rather than to inherent characteristics, and France's inability to retain Algeria can hardly be blamed on faulty doctrine. Whatever her policies or methods, France after 1954 could have maintained her dominance over Algeria only if the political system and intent of the country had been reshaped along totalitarian lines, and if her allies had become far less flexible in their dealings with the Communist powers. A totalitarian nation within the framework of an aggressively anti-Russian and anti-Chinese alliance might well have won the revolutionary war in Algeria.

It was, nevertheless, one of the great weaknesses of the doctrine of *guerre révolutionnaire* that it wrongly interpreted the relationship between the U.S.S.R., China, and the West in the post-Stalin era. Strategically, the doctrine made sense only in a world engaged in permanent war—a war, moreover, that excluded the possibility of mutual accommodation, or rifts between allies, that denied the existence of neutrals, and of balanced spheres of influence and power. In the eyes of the theorists, the Communist bloc had to be opposed by a monolithic France, to be reinforced eventually by an equally monolithic West. France stood in the van of this struggle, they claimed, because in Algeria she actually engaged the enemy, and because in Asia and Africa she had learned to appreciate the predominance of intellectual and moral factors over purely physical force. That the ideas of colonialism were no longer effective in the contemporary world they acknowledged; that neocolonial substitutes were no improvement they could scarcely admit so long as the concept of a French Algeria remained the basis for policy.[1]

The doctrine's imperial and colonial aspects severely weakened the doctrine itself during the fighting. They also limit the doctrine's application beyond Algeria. But the qualifications bearing on *guerre révolutionnaire* in its entirety need not extend to its various components. Some may prove effective in the future, at least in the defense against subversion in underdeveloped countries, if the policies they represent are more closely attuned to the political and psychological realities than they were in Algeria. At the same time, the incumbent authorities, and their foreign allies, must recognize that techniques, far from operating in a vacuum, possess political and social implications of their own. The resettlement or re-education of large numbers of people may weaken a guerrilla movement; but such programs, regardless of the sophistication and humanity with which they are carried out, will create new problems that must be solved. Difficult as the problems will be, distasteful as the involvement in another country's affairs may seem to its Western allies, governments will accept these implications if it becomes a matter of countering imminent danger. But antisubversive campaigns are holding operations. Their purpose, realistically considered, is to gain time, not to destroy the enemy. No conventional triumphant outcome can be expected, and the actions required to blunt the subversive threat should not be permitted to compromise the essential subsequent process of consolidation and reform.

In revolutionary wars, the integration of political and military measures that is a part of every war must not only determine the grand lines of strategy but also effectively inform the tactical decisions. The French met this requirement for all-encompassing, low-level integration by extending the responsibility of the armed forces even to those actions that were remote from combat in the traditional sense. But this is not the only possible answer. The last forty years have shown us cases of Communist as well as non-Communist revolutionary warfare that suggest that integration may be more effectively achieved by an extension not of military but of civilian authority. Those areas of internal war that, despite their military implications, are essentially social, economic, and political are perhaps more efficiently managed by civilians than by even the most thoroughly indoctrinated military personnel.

The role of civilians in revolutionary war remained, however, largely unexplored in Indochina and Algeria. The French experience, as well as the body of theorists and adherents of *guerre révolutionnaire,* was almost wholly military in character. This approach did not lead to satisfactory settlements in these conflicts, while pushing the country to the edge of revolution. The conclusion to be drawn was pointed out by a French officer in the new atmosphere after the "Week of the Barricades." He argued that although the armed forces could and should fight against the effects of subversion, they were neither organized nor equipped to combat the causes, and concluded: "To recognize that war has become total is implicitly to recognize that the Army can no longer handle more than a part of war."[2]

Appendix

Appendix

Center for Pacification and
Counterguerrilla Instruction

10th military region

USE OF THE PSYCHOLOGICAL ARM
IN THE ARMED FORCES

PART TWO: *PRINCIPLES OF ACTION*

    SECTION   I: BASIC PSYCHOLOGICAL PRINCIPLES
    SECTION   II: THE BASES OF DOCTRINE
    SECTION III: PLACE AND ROLE OF THE PSYCHO-
                LOGICAL-ACTION OFFICER
    SECTION IV: PROCEDURES

PART THREE: *PSYCHOLOGICAL ACTION ON THE*
                 TROOPS IN ALGERIA

    SECTION   I: OBJECTIVES
    SECTION   II: MILIEUS
    SECTION III: GENERAL ORDERS

Part One: GENERAL OBSERVATIONS

SECTION I: ROLE AND RESPONSIBILITY OF THE COMMAND

The Minister of National Defense and of the Armed Forces, assisted by the Chief of the General Staff of the Armed Forces, issues the directives and orders concerning the use of the psychological arm.

In *wartime operations,* the commanders in chief of the theaters of war are responsible for the use of the psychological arm in accordance with the directives received from the High Command.

The Commander of Interior Defense is responsible for the use of the psychological arm within the framework of his assigned mission.

In *pacification operations,* in which the armed forces are acting on request or by delegation of the civil power, the commander will receive individual directives from the civil authority responsible for the territory in which he is operating.

It is the concern of the commander, responsible at all times and in all circumstances for the use of the psychological arm as well as for the morale of the troops, to (1) see that subordinates are constantly imbued with the fundamental importance of these matters; (2) bring to the attention of superior echelons all information touching on the use of the psychological arm; and (3) forward every request or suggestion concerning actions that seem to him necessary and that he cannot handle with his own means.

In no case must organization interfere with the responsibility of command, which is total in this matter, or with the principle of Army unity, by creating a parallel hierarchy.

Section II: Use of the Psychological Arm in Interior Defense and in Pacification Operations

Article 1: General observations

Operations of interior defense and of pacification can become necessary in the event of a subversive war begun in metropolitan France or in overseas territory, whether or not this is supported from outside.

Subversive wars are generally waged according to the principles and methods of revolutionary war.

Revolutionary war is characterized by *its objective*, that is, physical and psychological control of the "masses" . . . ; *its techniques* of material and moral conquest of individuals with the aim of "popular mobilization" of all; *its ideology*, which is capable of inflaming the masses that are to be conquered and of gaining sympathy for the revolutionary movement; and *its evolution*, which progressively appeals to violence.

It successively combines all national activities, creates and multiplies revolutionary bases, which are strictly controlled, in order, finally, to launch a general political, psychological, and military offensive.

Article 2: Antisubversive action of the armed forces during periods of calm

The armed forces contribute to the checking of the development of subversive action. To this end, they devote a considerable effort to the civic and moral education of their personnel and to informing them of current affairs. They thus reach the families and relatives of this military personnel.

Especially overseas, the armed forces must exercise a policy of "presence" and maintain close contact with the populations, in particular during maneuvers, reconnaissances, raids, surprise attacks, etc. This policy presupposes numerous permanent personnel who are aware of their mission.

This contact is especially beneficial if the military units participate actively in local life and bring all possible help to the civil authorities and to the population in all areas—administration, public health, culture, sports, etc.

Such action also raises their own morale. It facilitates the mission of the "surveillance-protection" network set up by the security services.

Article 3: Role of the armed forces during periods of violence

The political authority determines the participation of the Army in pacification operations. During such operations, the armed forces face the difficulty of distinguishing between hostile, undecided, neutral, and weak elements.

The action of the armed forces can simultaneously cover two phases: (1) the destruction of the enemy organization; and (2) the rallying and organizing of dissident groups of the population and the protection of weak elements. In execution, these two phases are intimately linked and react upon each other.

The armed forces undertake the destruction of the politico-military organization that makes up the subversive structure on which hostile action is based. This armed-forces action, which aims at the known adversaries, the active members of the subversive organization, has meaning only if, at the same time, the rallying of the population puts an end to rebel recruiting.

The final goal is achieved by the elimination of enemy bases and their replacement by friendly bases—a result that can be obtained only by the cooperation of the great majority of the population. The struggle is essentially progressive. As it advances, it is reinforced by the establishment of stable administration, whose achievement will coincide with military victory.

Thus, the final goal of military operations is psychological.

To acquire or keep the moral support of the populations, it is necessary to: (1) offer an ideal capable of moving them or even of inflaming them; (2) discredit the hostile ideology by underscoring the contradictions between its principles and its acts; (3) act in ac-

cordance with the proposed ideal; (4) safeguard the interests of the
population; and (5) *organize the population* and develop its own
defense. This latter should not be imposed, but created by the
chief, requested by the population, and backed up by the armed
forces.

Psychological war and psychological action overlap closely in
the measures taken with regard to rebel elements. At the same time
that these elements are being destroyed, an attempt must be made
to separate them internally, to isolate them from the populations,
and to foment desertions, indeed, to recruit from among them.

For the execution of their tasks in periods of violence, the armed
forces have at their disposal all the specialized resources of the psychological arm. They should make the greatest possible use of
local manpower and resources.

In conclusion, the overlapping of the phases of these operations,
which has already been underscored, implies, toward the target,
respect for the principle of concentrating—rather than dispersing
—the resources of the psychological arm, and, in execution, decen-
tralization, since the *influence of each person who carries out these
operations is considerable.*

Section III: Psychological Action in the Armed Forces

Psychological action within the armed forces has as its objects: (1)
the creation, development, and maintenance of morale; and (2)
the "immunization" of personnel against hostile psychological attacks.

The psychological action to be undertaken is based on the
knowledge of the total situation and of the human relations
within the environment, and on an awareness of the moral implications at every stage of its development.

It acts upon the several internal components of morale: (1) individual conviction and the degree of adherence to the needs of
the nation, of the Army, and of the Army's mission; (2) the initial
degree of cohesion of units; (3) confidence in the leaders and in

the manner in which command is exercised; and (4) the character of group and individual ambitions, which are linked to the quality of the particular unit.

Article 1: Creation and development of morale

Creation of morale is basically achieved through civic instruction and patriotic education. Leaders should develop and complete this process, if necessary, and combine with it the traditional military values: discipline, military honor, and *esprit de corps*. To attain these values is the object of the psychological struggle.

Traditional military values should not be considered as the outcome of military factors alone. Adherence to them should be bolstered by argument and other appropriate means.

Discipline should be recognized as the very precondition of drive and effectiveness in every collective action, as the essential law that for each soldier reinforces the rules governing the life of the group. It is valueless to try to impose discipline upon the modern fighting man—frequently isolated—without seeking to awake his deepest loyalties.

Military honor is a way of life, at once individual and collective; it is a powerful cohesive factor. Despite the very difficult conditions of modern combat, the particular nature of psychological warfare, the difficulty of controlling the behavior of individuals and groups undergoing ordeals of all kinds and separated by combat, it remains the keystone of military education. . . .

SECTION IV: GENERAL OBSERVATIONS ON METHODS

Man, in his heart and mind, is the basic objective of psychological war and psychological action. For his emotional and intellectual conquest, propaganda will be effective only in so far as it is guided by the heart and the intelligence. This is why its use demands personal contact, which remains the best method of persuasion.

In psychological warfare, man is both the goal and the motive power of action.

To make contact with the human being who wears the enemy mask, the psychological arm will play upon the principles and instincts that are rooted in every individual. It will appeal to mass feeling, to collective and individual interests, and to the disagreements among the opposition.

Beliefs, principles, instincts should be exploited in psychological warfare, but never attacked directly. In psychological action, they are used as auxiliaries of the moral factors.

Since man is the principal and best actor in the psychological struggle, command must be constantly alert to make each member of the armed forces, in his own sphere, contribute to psychological action and, in certain cases, to psychological war. This contribution will increase the cohesiveness of units and will increase the effectiveness of the actions undertaken.

The execution of psychological action presupposes a common doctrinal base, whose elements are determined by the highest governmental and military direction, and the *full and entire support of the personnel to each and every mission.*

Part Two: PRINCIPLES OF ACTION

Section I: Basic Psychological Principles

Psychological action is based on man's most stable qualities, especially on common sense and reason, in order to affect positively the least stable ones. It strives to develop the critical spirit of each individual; it is directed toward making each individual a complete man and a citizen conscious of his rights and duties with respect to the national community; and it is a powerful factor in moral and civic education.

Section II: The Bases of Doctrine

The doctrine on which psychological action rests includes essentially an ideal of truth and liberty, of moral values and principles—

foundations of our conception of free men living within a given institutional framework. . . .

Institutions: Our ideal is embodied in the framework of three institutions: Nation, Homeland, and Army.

(1) Nation:

A community that has created its own unity.

A community with a desire to live together.

Citizenship is the awareness of the national reality and the recognition of the role and responsibility of every man within the country.

(2) Homeland:

A heritage that must be transmitted *in its entirety and with which we are not free to tamper.*

An association of individuals, a federation of families in a unique geographic, economic, historical, social, and cultural context.

"France, a wellspring of pride and traditions." (Paul Valéry)

A country in which it is "good to live"—more so than anywhere else in the world.

The role played by France in the world. Its great men, its discoveries, its accomplishments, its unusual reforms.

(3) Army:

The essential instrument of national defense.

The guardian of our liberty, the precondition for a free country.

The force that has permitted the creation and the preservation of France.

The melting pot for the youth of our country.

One of the greatest moral forces of the nation, carrying to their highest point the qualities of honor, courage, and disinterested service.

It is due to these institutions and it is in their framework that we can live according to our ideal. This bespeaks their importance. Everything must be done to defend them and to make them secure.

SECTION III: PLACE AND ROLE OF THE PSYCHOLOGICAL-ACTION OFFICER

"Corps commanders [and other commanding officers] are responsible, each within the area of his concern and according to instructions received from higher authority, for the morale of the men who are entrusted to them. They will take the necessary measures to act upon the morale of units or will propose these measures to higher authority" (D.M. 4802/EMFA/PS of October 4, 1955).

It follows from this that psychological action should not be restricted to specialists, but should inform the activities of every command.

"Every action is psychological." Nevertheless, the importance of this area requires the existence of some specialists: the morale and psychological-action officer, the information officer, the national-relations officer, the SSDN/FA officer, the social service.

Deeply convinced of his mission, the psychological-action officer is at once the counselor of the command, the instructor of the cadre, and the technician of modern procedures designed to create, for use by the units of the three services, the psychological arm in its offensive and defensive forms.

SECTION IV: PROCEDURES

Psychological action utilizes a certain number of distinct methods that can be employed separately or together. The principal method is *personal and direct verbal approach* by a leader in the role of moderator whose aim is to win over a unit to the opinions and the practical outlook for the future that he advances. This method can be backed up by indirect means, such as *written information,* or by various *audiovisual procedures.*

A. VERBAL APPROACH

This can take place either during special meetings or in the course of the daily routine. It can be addressed either to an isolated individual or to a group.

(1) *Private conference:* This is irreplaceable because it sets up a personal human contact. The leader must be able to use it to persuade a man to be interested in the life of the group and in its objectives, to change his attitude, to question him on his personal problems and to help him to resolve them, and to know his reactions.

(2) *Discussion meeting:* Directed toward a restricted group. Aims at having everyone take a stand on a theoretical or practical problem of concern to the group or its surroundings, and at gathering opinions and suggestions. Its purpose is to reinforce the cohesiveness of a group whose members already know one another, in order to make the group dynamic and influential.

The discussion meeting is very effective insofar as it demands personal reflection and the initiative of the participants. It is difficult to lead, however, and can result in confusion if the leader is not experienced enough.

(3) *The talk:* This is addressed to a fairly large group to inform it on a question of a general nature. It is easy to implement; every unit commander should know how to use it. Ideas to be retained should be repeated often.

B. WRITTEN INFORMATION. *The press, posters, and tracts.*

C. AUDIOVISUAL TECHNIQUES. *Films and the film club, film strips, radio and television, photomontages and drawings, singing, "sound and light" spectacles, dramatic presentations, information trips.*

Finally, the various elements of military symbolism or ceremonial (retreat, etc.), as well as the soldier's working equipment (arms, etc.), can serve as audiovisual aids.

Part Three: PSYCHOLOGICAL ACTION ON THE TROOPS IN ALGERIA

I. *Objectives:* The objectives are essentially to protect the morale of the troops against harmful propaganda; to raise this morale by giving the Army a "good conscience" and confidence; and to make each soldier a propagandist for the French cause in Algeria.

II. *Milieus:* The military milieu on which psychological action is to be brought to bear is, in actual fact, made up of individual milieus, each with different characteristics.

A distinction must be made among career soldiers, draftees, possibly those recalled to service, Africans, and the Moslem French of Algeria.

It is obvious that each of these milieus, because each responds to different concerns, motives, and characteristics, must be the object of different psychological actions.

III. *General Orders:* Certain general arrangements have been ordered by the command. These are weekly talks, information boards in units, distribution of the newspaper *Bled* and of documentation from the National Defense Information Service (Service d'Information de la Défense Nationale), the Regional Psychological Office (Bureau Psychologique Regional), and of films having to do with the Algerian question; listening to special broadcasts.

Notes

Notes

Chapter 1. Introduction

1. "La guerre révolutionnaire," talk on July 2, 1957, reprinted in *La défense nationale* (Paris, 1958), pp. 307–30.

2. *On War*, Book II, chap. ii.

3. Vincent Monteil, *Les Officiers* (Paris, 1958), p. 177.

4. No statistics can be established on this point. A senior officer with close friends in the psychological-warfare sections estimated early in 1961 that, among Army officers, at most 20 per cent wholly accepted the views of *guerre révolutionnaire* on modern war.

Chapter 2. The Doctrine: Revolution

1. Some French writers prefer to use "revolutionary war" to describe "the world-wide Communist movement of subversion and infiltration," and "subversive war" for the actual technique of taking over a nation from within. See for example, Colonel Rocolle's article, "Les constantes de la guerre subversive," *Revue de Défense Nationale*, XIV (February, 1958).

According to the sociologist Raoul Girardet, the official terminology of French military education defines "revolutionary war" as "a doctrine of war expounded by Marxist-Leninist theoreticians and exploited by revolutionary movements of various leanings." See his article, "Civil and Military Power in the Fourth Republic," in Samuel P. Huntington (ed.), *Changing Patterns of Military Politics* (New York, 1962), p. 148.

2. Colonel Georges Bonnet, *Les guerres insurrectionnelles et révolutionnaires* (Paris, 1958), p. 60.

3. The French Army distinguishes between "psychological action," directed toward safeguarding morale and ideological cohesion on the French side, and "psychological warfare," directed against the adversary. See Commandant Mairal-Bernard's article, "5ièmes bureaux et 7ième arme," *Revue des Forces Terrestres,* January, 1958.

4. "Ximenès," "La guerre révolutionnaire et ses données fondamentales," *Revue Militaire d'Information,* February–March, 1957, p. 8. This issue of 112 pages, with an introduction by Colonel Lacheroy, was wholly devoted to revolutionary warfare.

5. Cf. also the quotation in George Uhlmann's early article "Land of Five Withouts," *Far Eastern Survey,* XII, No. 9 (1943), 87: "The Army is like a school of fish and the people the water without which the fish can neither live nor move. Therefore the water must be free of obstacles and the temperature adapted to the life of the fish. It follows that the people must understand the reasons for the war."

6. Commandant J. Hogard, "Guerre révolutionnaire et pacification," *Revue Militaire d'Information,* January, 1957. Some of Commandant Hogard's colleagues have criticized his analysis for its rigidity (cf. also the *Revue's* editorial description of his article as "*très schématisé*"); it has, nevertheless, found very widespread acceptance in French military thought. For a more sophisticated version of Hogard's five phases, see pp. 265–70 in Colonel Louis Berteil's work *De Clausewitz à la guerre froide* (Paris, 1958).

7. "Un groupe d'officiers," "La guerre du Viet-Minh," *Revue Militaire d'Information* (February–March, 1957), p. 30.

8. "Ximenès," *op. cit.,* p. 17.

9. Wilfred Burchett, *North of the 17th Parallel* (Delhi, 1956), p. 140.

10. "La guerre révolutionnaire," *La défense nationale,* p. 322.

11. An interesting attempt to analyze and codify revolutionary wars throughout history has been undertaken by Colonel Georges Bonnet, whose approach is scholarly rather than doctrinaire. He argues that both weak and despotic regimes contain the germs of revolt; as causes, he distinguishes religious, economic, social, racial, and political antagonisms. To activate the causes, there must be a catalyzing agent, which may be an elite group, a charismatic leader, a conspiracy, or a secret society. The resulting conflicts are classified as civil wars, wars of liberation against a usurper or a foreign power, and counter-insurrections. See Bonnet's *Les guerres insurrectionnelles et révolutionnaires,* especially pp. 13–50.

12. General Nemo, "La guerre dans le milieu social," *Revue de Défense Nationale,* XII (May, 1956), 611.

13. *Ibid.,* p. 615.

14. No source is given for Hogard's statement that security of the rear constitutes "*le premier des principes de la guerre selon Lénine.*" Lenin's writings afford no indication that he singled out this "principle of war" above all others.

15. Hogard, *op. cit.*, pp. 12–13.
16. "Ximenès," *op. cit.*, p. 17.
17. Rocolle, *op. cit.*, p. 250.

Chapter 3. The Doctrine: Counterrevolution

1. Hogard, *op. cit.*, p. 15.
2. *Ibid.*, pp. 13–14.
3. The recognition of this fact of revolutionary life is shared by many observers, who otherwise have little in common with the French Army theorists. Germaine Tillion, for example, stated that "a resistance movement can be stamped out by annihilating all of its networks, no matter where they are—if one is ready to pay the price. But . . . these various political cells would simply start growing all over again soon after military defeat." Testimony presented at the trial of the FLN commander of the Algiers area, and reprinted in *Encounter*, December, 1958, p. 19.
4. For a representative expression of this point of view, see General Nemo, "A la recherche d'une doctrine," *Revue Militaire Générale*, March, 1958, pp. 345–46.
5. An excellent analysis of the relationship between Algerian nationalism and Communism can be found in Edward Behr, *The Algerian Problem* (New York, 1962), pp. 233–41.
6. The argument that Europe is in danger of imminent encirclement can be encountered very frequently in the writings of the theorists of *guerre révolutionnaire*. For a representative example, see the article by General L. M. Chassin, "Vers un encerclement de l'occident," *Revue de Défense Nationale*, XII (May, 1956). General Chassin sums up Russian grand strategy in three "directives by Khrushchev": "Develop maximum Communist infiltration in all of Africa; order all existing Communist organizations to put themselves at the disposal of nationalist movements; give complete support to all revolutionary movements, including those based on religious fanaticism." (P. 540.)
7. Speech of November 15, 1957. Large extracts of the speech have been published in Michel Déon, *L'Armée d'Algérie et la pacification* (Paris, 1959). This quotation is from pp. 7–8. General Allard expressed similar views in his article "L'OTAN et l'Afrique du nord," *Revue de Défense Nationale*, XIV (June, 1958).
8. The quotation is from a statement by M. Soustelle printed in *The Times* (London), December 3, 1958.
9. It may be noted that the vast bibliography of the theorists of *guerre révolutionnaire* does not contain a single serious monograph on the ideology of the FLN.
10. Raoul Girardet, "Civil and Military Power in the Fourth Republic," p. 133. It is interesting to note that this article was quoted by the defense counsel for General Challe at the trial of Challe and Zeller. M. Girardet himself was reported to be under arrest for some time in the summer of 1961.

11. "X," "Réponse aux partisans d'une petite France," *Revue de Défense Nationale*, XII (June, 1956), 684–85.

12. "Cette guerre de notre temps," *Revue de Défense Nationale*, XIV (August–September, 1958), 1317.

13. Quoted in Déon, *op. cit.*, pp. 77–79.

Chapter 4. The Components of Counterrevolutionary Warfare

1. Déon, *op. cit.*, p. 154.

2. Colonel Roger Trinquier in *La guerre moderne*, an important analysis of revolutionary warfare by an expert. An English translation, *Modern Warfare: A French View of Counterinsurgency* (New York, 1964), is now available and will be cited here. The quotation above is from p. 90.

3. These are very rough figures, useful only to indicate the proportions of the Army's division of labor. They do not include the gendarmerie and civilian police, which often closely supported the troops. Some Army, gendarmerie, and police personnel were organized into a permanent formation, the Détachment Opérationnel de Protection.

4. For the theory and practice of *quadrillage* during the French Revolution, see Peter Paret, *Internal War and Pacification: The Vendée, 1789–1796* (Research Monograph No. 12, Center of International Studies, Princeton University, 1961), p. 53.

5. General André Zeller at his trial in 1961. See the trial report, *Le procès des généraux Challe et Zeller* (Paris, 1961), p. 46.

6. Commandant Etcheverry in the April, 1958, issue of the service journal *Contacts*.

7. As Communists never ceased· to point out, the name of these units was derived from *Jagdkommandos*, German guerrilla pursuit formations that fought on the Eastern front and in the Balkans during World War II.

8. Directive 19/R.M. 10/3 I.N.S. of January 3, 1958.

9. Most of the information on native counterguerrilla groups is based on the chapter "Une riposte à la guerre révolutionnaire: les contre-maquis," in Déon, *op. cit.*, pp. 88–119.

10. *Contribution des français de souche nord-africaine à la pacification.* Pamphlet published by the French Press and Information Service, New York. I am grateful to Frank Wisner II for calling my attention to this work. At Challe's trial, one of his former subordinates, Colonel Boissieu, stated that in the summer of 1960, 45,000 Moslems served as regulars. *Le procès des généraux Challe et Zeller*, p. 143.

11. See the detailed report, *Des harkis et des hommes*, published as a special unnumbered and undated supplement by the journal *Témoignage Chrétien* in March, 1961.

12. *Contribution des français de souche nord-africaine à la pacification.*

Déon, *op. cit.*, p. 108, gives the following figures for harkas: 2,000 at the beginning of 1957; 26,100 on September 1, 1958; nearly 30,000 in January, 1959. In the summer of 1960, according to Boissieu, there were 60,000 harkas. (*Le procès des généraux Challe et Zeller*, p. 143.) Not included in these statistics are the volunteers of European descent, who had been organized into so-called Unités Territoriales at the end of 1955. From a simple militia with police and guard duties, the UT quickly developed into the armed force of the Algerian ultras, acquiring a staff organization and heavy weapons, including Sherman tanks. By the beginning of 1960, their total strength was estimated at 110,000, which was greater than the number of Moslem auxiliaries. The UT constituted the prime force in the insurrection of January, 1960, contributing more than half of the contingent on the Algiers barricades. On February 10, the government disbanded them.

13. *Le procès des généraux Challe et Zeller*, pp. 40–41.

14. Paret, *Internal War and Pacification*, p. 54.

15. A. Souyris, "Un procédé efficace de contre-guérilla: L'auto-défense des populations," *Revue de Défense Nationale*, XII (June, 1956). A translation appeared in the *Military Review*, March, 1957.

16. *Le procès des généraux Challe et Zeller*, p. 143. See also Challe's statement, *ibid.*, p. 29.

17. Déon, *op. cit.*, p. 135.

18. Trinquier, *op. cit.*, p. 74.

19. For an informative though overenthusiastic account of the operation, see the article by General Desjours, "La pacification dans le secteur de Blida," *Revue des Forces Terrestres*, October, 1959.

20. The figure is given in a statement by Jean Morin, Delegate-General of the Government in Algeria, printed in *Le Monde*, June 18–19, 1961. As early as February, 1960, an English observer estimated the number of displaced persons as close to 1,500,000 in camps and settlements, with another 500,000 migrants in Morocco and the Algerian towns "where they create new *bidonvilles* as fast as the authorities can dispose of the old ones." See the article "Efforts to resettle the Muslims of Algeria," *The Times* (London), February 23, 1960.

21. *Contribution des français de souche nord-africaine à la pacification.*

22. On the history of the Bureaux Arabes, see the article by General M. Boucherie, "Les Bureaux Arabes: Leur rôle dans la conquête de l'Algérie," *Revue de Défense Nationale*, XIII (July, 1957).

23. A Bureau Arabe was made up of a commanding officer, his second-in-command, a physician, an interpreter, a native judge, secretaries and native auxiliaries, and a platoon of spahis commanded by a French lieutenant. Boucherie, *op. cit.*, p. 1057.

24. General Partiot, "Organisation et activité des S.A.S.," interview published in *Service d'Information* (Algiers), May 24, 1960.

25. Letter published under the heading "Les S.A.S. et les maires d'Algérie," in *Le Monde*, September 23, 1959.

26. *Rapport sur l'activité de l'administration*, published by the Délégation Générale du Gouvernement en Algérie (Algiers, 1959), p. 52. Of the officers,

834 were regulars, the 453 others reservists. Their tour of duty usually lasted three years.

27. There were some exceptions. Jules Roy, in his article "Rétour à Toudja," in *L'Express*, May 10, 1962, writes of an SAS captain whose proper place would have been at the head of a disciplinary camp.

Chapter 5. Psychological Action—Psychological Warfare

1. M. Mégret, *L'Action psychologique* (Paris, 1959), pp. 10, 90–91. I am much indebted to this well-informed, objective study.

2. These lectures were far from claiming exceptional power for psychological methods. Mégret, *op. cit.*, pp. 114–15, points out that as late as 1954, AP stressed the potential dangers to a democracy of intensive propaganda and indoctrination.

3. J. Planchais, "La 'septième arme' doit-elle rester l'apanage des militaires?" *Le Monde*, August 23, 1958.

4. See also the official directive on psychological action issued by the Center for Pacification and Counterguerrilla Instruction in Algeria and reprinted in the Appendix to this book.

5. Commandant Mairal-Bernard, *op. cit.*, p. 79.

6. Captain A. Souyris, "Réalité et aspects de la guerre psychologique," *Revue Militaire d'Information*, No. 302 (February, 1959), see especially pp. 20–23. See also the "Instruction sur les fondements, but et limites de l'action psychologique," issued by Pierre Guillaumat, Minister of the Armies, on July 28, 1959, and printed in *Le Monde*, October 3, 1959.

7. Peter Paret, "A Total Weapon of Limited War," *Journal of the Royal United Service Institution*, CV (February, 1960), 66.

8. On the psychological theories of *guerre révolutionnaire*, see especially M. Mégret, *La guerre psychologique* (Paris, 1956); Jean-Marie Domenach, "L'armée en république," *Esprit*, November, 1958; and the already cited articles by Captain Souyris and Commandant Mairal-Bernard, as well as Paret, "A Total Weapon of Limited War."

9. The original French version of Chakhotin's book, *Le viol des foules par la propagande politique*, was published in Paris in 1939 and quickly achieved five editions. The English translation, dedicated to H. G. Wells, "Thinker of the Future," appeared in London the same year, and is cited here.

10. Chakhotin, *op. cit.*, p. xvii.

11. *Ibid.*, pp. 284–85.

12. The companies were also called CDP (*compagnies de diffusion et production*).

13. Mairal-Bernard, *op. cit.*, p. 89. For an example of their work during a military operation, see Chapter 6 of this book.

14. J. Planchais, *L'Armée* (Paris, 1959), p. 55. A peak circulation of 350,000

copies is mentioned by George A. Kelly in "Revolutionary Warfare and Psychological Action," in Franklin Mark Osanka (ed.), *Modern Guerrilla Warfare: Fighting Communist Guerrilla Movements, 1941–1961* (New York, 1962), p. 435.

15. In an interview in 1958, the editors told me that the issue of February–March, 1957, which had been devoted entirely to *guerre révolutionnaire*, achieved a total printing of 48,000 copies.

16. The two types were not always separated. For example, the camp at Tigzirt in the Grand Kabyle, was a *camp de triage et de rééducation*. A considerable variety of stockades and of police and military jails also existed.

17. Déon, *op. cit.*, p. 112. This routine was not followed invariably. Members of the "White" category often ended up in the camps, as did acquitted prisoners, for example, Aissat Idir, the Secretary General of the Algerian Labor Unions (Unions Générales des Travailleurs Algériens, or UGTA), who was re-arrested in the courtroom and returned to the transit center at Birtraria, where he died after a few months in circumstances that have not yet been clarified.

18. See for example the estimates by Jacques Duquesne, an editor of the moderate Catholic newspaper *La Croix*, in his book *L'Algérie ou la guerre des mythes* (Bruges, 1958), p. 30. In 1957, an investigating team of the *Commission internationale contre le régime concentrationnaire* found 1,914 internees in one camp alone.

19. The *Notice sur l'Action Psychologique dans les Centres d'Hébergement* was published in several newspapers at the beginning of 1958, for example in the January 23 issue of *Le Monde*. Excerpts are also printed in Duquesne, *op. cit.*, pp. 32–33.

20. Déon, *op. cit.*, p. 111.

21. "Témoignage d'un combattant," by the commander of an SAS team, published in *Le Monde*, July 6, 1960.

22. Parts of the study were released to the press on April 24, 1959.

23. The report was published in the Catholic weekly *Témoignage Chrétien*, April 9, 1959. A translation appeared in *The Manchester Guardian*, April 10, 1959.

24. See the statement of Edmond Michelet, the Minister of Justice, in an interview published in *Le Monde* on December 2, 1959: "The camps are not my responsibility. This problem of the camps—why should I deny it?—is a worrisome one."

25. A full summary of the report appeared in *Le Monde*, January 4, 1960. Publication was unauthorized, but the genuineness of the text was denied neither by the Red Cross nor by the government. The issue of *Le Monde* carrying the report was confiscated in Algeria on the grounds that the summary contained operational information, rendered future visits of the Red Cross more difficult, and compromised the efforts of the authorities to bring order to the internment centers and to find abuses and repress them. On January 4, too, the Premier's office issued a communiqué that deplored the publication of the text, and went on to comment that while the report showed that "mistakes or abuses continue to be committed occasionally," it emphasized that

"very distinct improvement has been achieved." Two days later the editor of *Le Monde* defended the "grave indiscretion" of which his paper had been accused, and continued: "The regrettable and painful facts to which attention has often been called, but which have always been denied or contested, now become incontestable." In this connection, see also the long discussion of the action of the International Red Cross in Algeria since 1955 that appeared in *Le Monde* on February 12, 1960.

26. Reported in *Le Monde*, June 7, 1960.

27. The truth is, wrote *Témoignage Chrétien* on June 26, 1959, in a discussion of the suppressed pamphlet *Gangrène*, "torture will never be conquered as long as the war lasts . . . this is universally understood. General de Gaulle knows it; M. Debré knows it; M. Michelet knows and says it."

28. "Les conditions de la parade et de la riposte à la guerre révolutionnaire," *Revue Militaire d'Information*, February–March, 1957, p. 96.

29. Reprinted in *Le Monde*, August 5, 1959.

30. See the report of the trial in the Manchester *Guardian* of August 3, 1962. M. Max Lejeune, the Socialist Minister of the Army during the Battle of Algiers, has repeatedly denied that an order to use torture was ever given, stating that "the few isolated cases of torture were always punished." See particularly the interview with him in *Le Monde*, August 2, 1962.

31. International law and the laws of war are being intolerably strained by contemporary forms of irregular and internal war; but there is no doubt that under present rules French forces in Algeria were guilty of massive infractions. As a party to the Geneva Red Cross Conventions of 1949, France undertook to treat humanely any person not actively involved in the hostilities, including members of armed forces who had laid down their arms or who were *hors de combat*. Article 3 of the Conventions prohibits absolutely cruel treatment and torture, and since these rules extend to armed conflicts of a noninternational character, this obligation applies whether or not the opponent is recognized as a belligerent. It was, incidentally, a French delegate at the Diplomatic Geneva Conference who argued that these rules should be obeyed even against criminals.

32. Though strictly forbidden, the exhibiting of captured or killed rebels to the population was for years a favorite psychological-warfare technique.

33. Letter to *Preuves* of October, 1957.

34. Letter to *L'Express* of July 6, 1960, by the Abbé de Cossé-Brissac. The writer, member of one of the oldest and most distinguished French military families, saw the Dijon church in which he served as curé put out of bounds to soldiers in uniform by the local commanding general.

35. An interesting attempt to separate the bulk of the French forces from the torturers were the statements, appearing for years in the world press, that maltreatment was mainly the work of German members of the Foreign Legion.

36. Compare the already cited article by Souyris, "Réalité et aspects de la guerre psychologique," *Revue Militaire d'Information*, February, 1959.

37. See the communiqué issued by the Council of Ministers on February 10, 1960, and the subsequent circular of the Army Chief of Staff, General Demetz.

Chapter 6. The Doctrine in Action: Opération Pilote

1. The report, *Etude sur l'opération "Pilote" dans le Dahra oranais*, signed by Colonel Cazelles, Commanding Officer of the 5th Cavalry Brigade and of the Sector of Dahra, is classified No. 1062/50B.C./EM./S. and dated September 26, 1958. Barring some minor cuts and the omission of several appendixes, it is here translated in full. Editorial additions are in square brackets; lettered footnotes are part of the French original.

2. See for example, Déon, *op. cit.*, pp. 154–58.

3. "L'Armée française et la stratégie du F.L.N. en 1960," *La Nouvelle Critique*, January, 1961.

4. *Le Monde*, July 8, 1960.

5. *Le Figaro*, June 14, 1960.

6. Marcel Bigeard and Marc Flament, *Aucune bête au monde* . . . (Paris, 1959), p. 7.

7. *Le Figaro*, September 23, 1960.

8. In December, 1959, approximately 900,000 regulars, reservists, naval and air-force personnel, gendarmes, police, *gardes mobiles*, territorials and native auxiliaries were on the rolls as serving in Algeria. This total, which includes 158,813 native auxiliaries, is unrealistically high, and of course does not take account of great differences in reliability and training. These figures are based on *La Vie Militaire*, December 25, 1959, and on supplementary French information.

Chapter 7. Sources and Implications

1. Chassin, "Insuffisance de la stratégie nucléaire," *Revue de Défense Nationale*, XVI (July, 1960), 1194, 1198–99.

2. For example, such articles appeared in the *Military Review*, published by the U.S. Army Command and General Staff College, in 1957, 1958, and 1962.

3. Aron goes on to say that the conclusions "were dangerous because they were partly correct. The impossibility of winning certain colonial wars was not recognized, but violently denied, parliament and the intellectuals serving as scapegoats." See his book *L'Algérie et la république* (Paris, 1958), p. 91.

4. The French literature on the new colonial warfare is vast. The most useful works are those written by the leading practitioners; for example, J. S. Gallieni, *La pacification de Madagascar* (Paris, 1900); C. Mangin, *Souvenirs d'Afrique* (Paris, 1936); L. de Grandmaison, *En territoire militaire* (Paris, 1899); H. G. Lyautey, *Paroles d'action* (Paris, 1927); the same author's *Lettres du sud de Madagascar* (Paris, 1935); and especially his seminal article "Du rôle colonial de l'armée," in the *Revue des Deux Mondes* of January 15, 1900. An excellent objective study is H. Brunschwig's *La colonisation française* (Paris, 1949). The most accessible English treatment is J. Gottmann's chapter "Bugeaud, Gallieni, Lyautey: The Development of French Colonial

Warfare," in the repeatedly reprinted volume *Makers of Modern Strategy*, ed. E. M. Earle (Princeton, 1943); but it is uncritical and should be read with caution.

5. Lyautey, *Lettres du sud de Madagascar*, p. 164.

6. Lyautey, "Du rôle colonial de l'armée," pp. 312–13.

7. *Ibid.*, p. 310.

8. General Huré, "Stratégie et tactique marocaines," *Revue des Questions de Défense Nationale*, I, No. 3 (July, 1939), 397–412.

9. "Du Rôle social de l'officier dans le service militaire universel," *Revue des Deux Mondes*, CIV (March 15, 1891). See also R. Girardet, *La société militaire dans la France contemporaine (1815–1939)* (Paris, 1953), pp. 279–311.

10. J. Fauvet and J. Planchais in their excellent book, *La fronde des généraux* (Paris, 1961), pp. 68–69.

11. *Ibid.*, pp. 69–70. In the quotation, "radical" should be taken in its French meaning, i.e., slightly left of center.

12. W. Bosworth, *Catholicism and Crisis in Modern France: French Catholic Groups at the Threshold of the 5th Republic* (Princeton, 1962), pp. 183–84. Whether Sauge was actually a member of the Communist Party is open to doubt. On his career, and on the involvement of Catholic extremists in the various "antisubversive" movements of the 1950's, see the valuable article by J. Maître, "Le Catholisme d'extrême-droite et la croisade antisubversive," *Revue Française de Sociologie*, April–June, 1961.

13. "Until these last months," A. Jacob wrote in *Le Monde*, February 12, 1960, "M. Georges Sauge was the official theoretician of *l'action psychologique*."

14. The description is Raoul Girardet's. See p. 27 of this book.

15. Zeller, "Armée et politique," *Revue de Défense Nationale*, XIII (April, 1957), 514. The article contains several such warnings and challenges to the government, but seems not to have been taken seriously at the time. Not surprisingly, at Zeller's trial for his participation in the insurrection of 1961, passages of the article were incorporated in the final statement of the prosecution.

16. Apart from the conflict between Frenchmen in occupied and Vichy France, there were several occasions of relatively sizable internecine fighting, for example, in Syria during June and July, 1941, when 2,000 Frenchmen were killed.

17. When he heard that police were searching for him, General Chassin is supposed to have cried, "They are pushing me into illegality!" See Merry and Serge Bromberger, *Les 13 complots du 13 Mai* (Paris, 1959), p. 209.

18. Fauvet and Planchais, *op. cit.*, p. 66.

19. See *ibid.*, p. 65, where the authors go so far as to suggest that the colonels who masterminded the April, 1961 rebellion were "intoxicated intoxicators"— themselves victims of the internal logic of the theories they had adopted.

20. See Chapter 4, n. 2.

21. Roger Trinquier, *Pour vaincre . . . la guérilla et le terrorisme*, "Avant Propos," a mimeographed early version of *La guerre moderne*, circulated within the services.

22. *Ibid.*

23. In the fall of 1958, the pamphlet was reprinted as a document of contemporary interest by the well-known Parisian military publishers Berger-Levrault. All quotations refer to this edition.

24. *Contre-révolution, stratégie et tactique*, pp. 87–91.

25. *Ibid.*, p. 16.

26. *Ibid.*, p. 17.

27. *Ibid.*, p. 23.

28. *Ibid.*, p. 34.

29. *Ibid.*, p. 56.

30. *Ibid.*, p. 56.

31. *Ibid.*, p. 56.

32. *Ibid.*, pp. 101–2.

33. *Ibid.*, p. 132.

34. *Le Problème algérien—solution française. L'Express*, May 10, 1962, printed excerpts of Argoud's pamphlet, from which the present quotations are taken.

35. J.-M. Domenach, "The French Army in Politics," *Foreign Affairs*, XXXIX, No. 2 (January, 1961), 189. See also such characteristic reports as A. Jacob's in *Le Monde*, September 22, 1959, headed: "*Chefs de poste ou de S.A.S. se sentent liés par les promesses faites aux populations qu'ils administrent.*"

36. Domenach, "The French Army in Politics," p. 194.

Chapter 8. Conclusion

1. After a lost war, governments and political movements often stress the value of abstract and psychological forces, perhaps in an attempt to make up for the loss in military and economic strength. This attitude sometimes becomes the basis for a revolution or "national regeneration." General de Gaulle, who has never conceded the defeat or the weakness of France, characteristically discounts the importance of the psychological services; instead, he places his trust in the conventional concepts of an active foreign policy coupled to a strong military establishment, i.e., one that today includes a nuclear capability.

2. Lieutenant Colonel J. Rousset, "A propos de subversion et d'insurrection," *Revue de Défense Nationale*, XVI (March, 1960), 506.

A Select Bibliography
of Writings on
Guerre Révolutionnaire

A Select Bibliography
of Writings on
Guerre Révolutionnaire

I. THEORY

ALLARD, J. "L'OTAN et l'Afrique du nord," *Revue de Défense Nationale*, XIV (June, 1958).

ALQUIER, J. Y. *Nous avons pacifié Tazalt*. Paris, 1957.
An informative account of the SAS.

ANONYMOUS. *Contre-révolution: Stratégie et tactique*. Paris, 1958.

ARGOUD, A. *Le problème algérien—solution française*. Published by the Direction Centrale of the Organisation Armée Secrète, n.d.

BAILLIF, GEN. "Forces armées et psychologie," *Revue de Défense Nationale*, XVI (May, 1960).

BERTEIL, L. *De Clausewitz à la guerre froide*. Paris, 1958.

BONNET, G. *Les guerres insurrectionnelles et révolutionnaires*. Paris, 1958.

———. "Mao Tsé-Toung et la stratégie révolutionnaire," *Revue de Défense Nationale*, XI (January, 1955).

BRYGOO, R. "Les armées nationales et la difficile mission du maintien de l'ordre," *Revue Militaire Générale*, January, 1960.

CAVAGNES. "Les opérations de maintien de l'ordre," *Revue Militaire Générale*, July, 1960.

CHAPELLE, GEN. DE LA. "Les aspects particuliers de la guerre possible," *Revue de Défense Nationale,* XII (February, 1956).

CHASSIN, L. M. "Du rôle historique de l'armée," *Revue de Défense Nationale,* XII (October, 1956).

———. "Insuffisance de la stratégie nucléaire," *Revue de Défense Nationale,* XVI (July, 1960).

———. *La conquête de la Chine par Mao Tsé-Toung (1945–1949).* Paris, 1952.

———. "Technique de l'insurrection," *Revue de Défense Nationale,* XIII (May, 1957).

———."Vers un encerclement de l'occident," *Revue de Défense Nationale,* XII (May, 1956).

DELMAS, C. "Entretien avec le général Challe," *Revue de Défense Nationale,* XVII (April, 1961).

———. *La guerre révolutionnaire.* Paris, 1959.

———. "Notes sur les fondements d'une doctrine de défense nationale," *Revue de Défense Nationale,* XIV (June, 1958).

———. "La rébellion algérienne après l'arrestation des chefs du F.L.N.," *Revue de Défense Nationale,* XII (December, 1956).

———. "Poignard ou bombe atomique," *Revue Militaire Générale,* May, 1959.

ELY, P. "L'Armée dans la nation," *Revue Militaire d'Information,* No. 297 (August, 1958).

———. "Les problèmes français et l'équilibre mondial," *Revue de Défense Nationale,* XV (November, 1959).

———. "Notre politique militaire," *Revue de Défense Nationale,* XIII (July, 1957).

———. "Perspectives stratégiques d'avenir," *Revue de Défense Nationale,* XIV (August, 1958).

Guide de l'officier des affaires algériennes. Service d'Information. Paris, 1957.

ENCAUSSE, H. "La 'persuasion' des consciences—méthodes de propagande soviétique," *Revue Militaire d'Information,* No. 282 (April, 1957).

HOGARD, J. "Cette guerre de notre temps," *Revue de Défense Nationale,* XIV (August–September, 1958).

———. "L'Armée française devant la guerre révolutionnaire," *Revue de Défense Nationale,* XIII (January, 1957).

———. "Guerre révolutionnaire et pacification," *Revue Militaire d'Information,* No. 280 (January, 1957).

———. "Guerre révolutionnaire ou révolution dans l'art de guerre," *Revue de Défense Nationale,* XII (December, 1956).

——. "Le soldat dans la guerre révolutionnaire," *Revue de Défense Nationale,* XIII (February, 1957).

LACHEROY, C. *Action Viêt-Minh et communiste en Indochine, ou une leçon de "guerre révolutionnaire."* Paris, 1955. [Mimeographed.]

——. "La guerre révolutionnaire," in *La défense nationale.* Paris, 1958.

——. *Scénario-type de guerre révolutionnaire.* Paris, 1955. [Mimeographed.]

——. *Une armée du Viêt-Minh: Les hiérarchies parallèles.* Paris, 1954. [Mimeographed.]

LACROIX, R. "L'emploi des hélicoptères n'est-il justifié qu'en Algérie?" *Revue de Défense Nationale,* XIV (May, 1958).

MAIRAL-BERNARD. "5ièmes bureaux et 7ième arme," *Revue des Forces Terrestres,* January, 1958.

METZ, DE. "Du rôle national de l'officier," *Revue de Défense Nationale,* XIV (August–September, 1958).

"MILITES." "Enquête sur la défense nationale," *Hommes et Mondes,* May, 1955.

NEMO, J. M. *En Indochine: Guérilla et contre-guérilla.* Paris, 1952. [Mimeographed.]

——. "The Place of Guerrilla Action in War," *Military Review,* XXXVII (November, 1957).

——. "A la recherche d'une doctrine," *Revue Militaire Générale,* March, 1958.

——. "La guerre dans le milieu social," *Revue de Défense Nationale,* XII (May, 1956).

——. "La guerre dans la foule," *Revue de Défense Nationale,* XII (June, 1956).

——. "La France et l'Afrique," *Revue de Défense Nationale,* XV (December, 1959), XVI (January–February, 1960).

PARTIOT, GEN. *Organisation et activité des S.A.S.* Service d'Information. Algiers, 1960.

PERRET-GENTIL, J. "L'armée française face à la guerre subversive," *L'Armée–La Nation,* XIII (October–November–December, 1959) and XV (May, 1960).

POIRIER, L. "Un instrument de guerre révolutionnaire: le F.L.N.," *Revue Militaire d'Information,* No. 289 (December, 1957) and No. 290 (January, 1958).

ROCOLLE, COL. "Les constantes de la guerre subversive," *Revue de Défense Nationale,* XIV (February, 1958).

ROCQUIGNY, COL. DE. "Urban Terrorism," *Military Review,* XXXVIII (February, 1959).

Souyris, A. "Les conditions de la parade et de la riposte à la guerre révolutionnaire," *Revue Militaire d'Information,* No. 281 (February–March, 1957).

———. "Réalité et aspects de la guerre psychologique," *Revue Militaire d'Information,* No. 302 (February, 1959).

———. "Un procédé efficace de contre-guérilla: L'auto-défense des populations," *Revue de Défense Nationale,* XII (June, 1956). Published in English as "An Effective Counterguerrilla Procedure," *Military Review,* XXXVI (March, 1957).

Thillaud. "Vaincre sans trahir," *Revue de Défense Nationale,* XIV (April, 1958).

Trinquier, R. *Modern Warfare: A French View of Counterinsurgency.* Translated by Daniel Lee. With an Introduction by Bernard B. Fall. New York, 1964.

———. Pour vaincre . . . la guérilla et le terrorisme. n.d. [Mimeographed.]

"X." Réponse aux partisans d'une petite France," *Revue de Défense Nationale,* XII (June, 1956).

"Ximenès," Souyris, A., *et al.* "La guerre révolutionnaire et ses données fondamentales," *Revue Militaire d'Information,* No. 281 (February–March, 1957).

Zeller, A. "Armée et politique," *Revue de Défense Nationale,* XIII (April, 1957).

II. BACKGROUND, ANALYSIS, CRITICISM

Alleg, H. *La question.* Paris, 1958.

Anonymous. "L'armée française et la stratégie du F.L.N. en 1960," *La Nouvelle Critique,* January, 1961.

Aron, R. *L'Algérie et la république.* Paris, 1958.

Azeau, H. *Révolte militaire.* Paris, 1961.

An excellent analysis of the motives underlying the "generals' revolt," which should be read with the equally good but more matter-of-fact account by Jacques Fauvet and Jean Planchais.

Barberot, R. *Malaventure en Algérie avec le général Paris de Bollardière.* Paris, 1957.

Bedjaoui, M. *La révolution algérienne et le droit.* With an Introduction by Pierre Cot. Brussels, 1961.

Behr, E. *The Algerian Problem.* New York, 1962.

An objective, informed account, as good on the military as on the political side.

BIGEARD, M., and FLAMANT, M. *Aucune bête au monde.* ... Paris, 1959. These combat photographs and their accompanying text constitute an impressive example of the mystique of duty and suffering, propagated by the adherents of *guerre révolutionnaire.*

BOSWORTH, W. *Catholicism and Crisis in Modern France.* Princeton, 1962.

BOUCHERIE, M. "Les bureaux arabes: Leur rôle dans la conquête de l'Algérie," *Revue de Défense Nationale,* XIII (July, 1957).

BROMBERGER, M. and S. *Les 13 complots du 13 mai.* Paris, 1959.

BROMBERGER, S. *Les rebelles algériens.* Paris, 1958.

BROMBERGER, S. and M., ELGEY, G. and CHAUVEL, J.-F. *Barricades et colonels.* Paris, 1960.

BROWN, B. E. "The Army and Politics in France," *Journal of Politics,* May, 1961.

BRUNSCHWIG, H. *La colonisation française.* Paris, 1949.

———. *Mythes et réalités de l'imperialisme coloniale française, 1871–1914.* Paris, 1960.

BURCHETT, W. *North of the 17th Parallel.* Delhi, 1956.

CHASSIN, L. M. "Guerre en Indochine," *Revue de Défense Nationale,* July, 1953.

CHEZAL, GUY DE. *Parachute en Indochine.* Paris, 1947.

CLARK, M. K. *Algeria in Turmoil.* New York, 1959. A partisan, anti-FLN account.

DARBOISE, J.-M., HEYNAUD, M., and MARTEL, J. *Officiers en Algérie.* Paris, 1960.

DÉON, M. *L'Armée d'Algérie et la pacification.* Paris, 1959. An able account by an author virulently opposed to Algerian independence.

DESJOURS, J. "La pacification dans le secteur de Blida," *Revue des Forces Terrestres,* October, 1959.

DOMENACH, J.-M. "The French Army in Politics," *Foreign Affairs,* XXXIX, No. 2 (January, 1961).

DRESCH, J., *et al. La question algérienne.* Paris, 1958.

DUQUESNE, J. *L'Algérie ou la guerre des mythes.* Bruges, 1958. An excellent critique of French policies in Algeria by the editor of the semiofficial Catholic daily *La Croix.*

FALL, B. B. *Le Viet Minh, 1945–1960.* Paris, 1960.

———. *Street Without Joy: Insurgency in Indochina, 1946–1963.* 3d rev. ed. Harrisburg, Pa. 1963. Contains interesting firsthand observations on the tactics used by both sides.

FAUVET, J., and PLANCHAIS, J. *La fronde des généraux.* Paris, 1961.

GALLIENI, J. S. *La pacification de Madagascar.* Paris, 1900.

Gangrène. With an Introduction by P. BENENSON. London, 1959.

GILLESPIE, J. *Algeria: Rebellion and Revolution.* New York, 1960.

GIRARDET, R. "Civil and Military Power in the Fourth Republic," in S. P. HUNTINGTON (ed.), *Changing Patterns of Military Politics.* New York, 1962.

GOTTMANN, J. "Bugeaud, Gallieni, Lyautey: The Development of French Colonial Warfare," in E. M. EARLE (ed.), *Makers of Modern Strategy.* 6th ed. Princeton, 1960.
A convenient if uncritical summary of some important French ideas on colonial warfare.

HUNTINGTON, S. P. "Patterns of Violence in World Politics," in S. P. HUNTINGTON (ed.), *Changing Patterns of Military Politics.* New York, 1962.

HURÉ, GEN. "Stratégie et tactique marocaines," *Revue des Questions de Défense Nationale,* I (July, 1939).
An informative article on the historical background of French operational techniques.

JEANSON, C. and F. *L'Algérie hors la loi.* Paris, 1955.
One of the earliest French condemnations of the Algerian War.

KATZENBACH, E. L., JR., "Indo-China: A Military-Political Appreciation," *World Politics,* IV (January, 1952).

KELLY, G. A. "Revolutionary War and Psychological Action," in F. M. OSANKA (ed.), *Modern Guerrilla Warfare.* New York, 1962.

KERAMANE, H. *La pacification.* Lausanne, 1960.
A detailed and sometimes documented account of atrocities purportedly committed by French forces in Algeria.

KRAFT, J. *The Struggle for Algeria.* New York, 1961.
A good general history of the Algerian War up to the Evian Conference.

LACOUTURE, J., and DEVILLERS, P. *La fin d'une guerre (Indochine 1954).* Paris, 1960.

LANIEL, J. *Le drame indochinois.* Paris, 1957.
This work by a former Prime Minister, which should be read together with General Navarre's apologia, includes an interesting chapter on the military faults of the campaign.

LAVISSE, E. "Une méthode coloniale: L'armée et la colonisation," *Revue de Paris,* June, 1899.

Le procès des généraux Challe et Zeller. Paris, 1961.
This and the following volume contain the stenographic reports of the trials.

Le procès du général Raoul Salan. Paris, 1962.

LYAUTEY, H. G. "Du rôle colonial de l'armée," *Revue des Deux Mondes,* January 15, 1900.

———. "Du rôle social de l'officier," *Revue des Deux Mondes*, March 15, 1891.

MÉGRET, M. "Crise du service militaire: les chemins de l'Algérie," *Revue de Défense Nationale*, XIII (January, 1957).

———. *L'action psychologique*. Paris, 1959.

———. *La guerre psychologique*. Paris, 1956.

MONTEIL, V. *Les Officiers*. Paris, 1958.
A useful introduction to the history and contemporary condition of the French officer corps.

NAVARRE, H. *L'Agonie de l'Indochine*. Paris, 1957.

PARET, P. "A Total Weapon of Limited War," *Journal of the Royal United Service Institution*, CV (February, 1960).

———. Review of COLONEL G. BONNET, *Les guerres insurrectionnelles et révolutionnaires*, in *Survival*, I (May–June, 1959).

———. "The French Army and La Guerre Révolutionnaire," *Journal of the Royal United Service Institution*, CIV (February, 1959).

PARET, P., and SHY, J. W. *Guerrillas in the 1960's*. New York, 1962.

PLANCHAIS, J. *L'Armée*. Paris, 1959.

———. *Le malaise de l'armée*. Paris, 1958.
Two informative, objective studies by the military editor of *Le Monde*.

RIESSEN, R. *Jungle Mission*. New York, 1957.

ROUSSET, J. "A propos de subversion et d'insurrection," *Revue de Défense Nationale*, XVI (March, 1960).

ROY, J. *La bataille dans la rizière*. Paris, n.d.

———. *Le métier des armes*. Paris, 1948.

———. "Retour à Toudja," *L'Express*, May 10, 1962.

———. *The War in Algeria*. New York, 1961.
A brief, brilliantly written condemnation of the war by a retired colonel and third generation French-Algerian.

SERVAN-SCHREIBER, J.-J. *Lieutenant en Algérie*. Paris, 1957.

SOTO, J. DE. "Pouvoir civil et pouvoir militaire," in *La défense nationale*. Paris, 1958.

SOUSTELLE, J. *Le drame algérien et la décadence française*. Paris, 1957.

TANHAM, G. *Communist Revolutionary Warfare*. New York, 1961.
An informative analysis of Vietminh organization, strategy, and tactics.

TILLION, G. "The Terrorist," *Encounter*, December, 1958.

VIDAL-NAQUET, P. *L'Affaire Audin*. Paris, 1958.

VO NGUYEN GIAP. *Dien Bien Phu*. Hanoi, 1959.

White Paper on the Application of the Geneva Conventions of 1949 to the French-Algerian Conflict. Issued by the Algerian Office, New York, 1960.